Comfort Food
ESSENTIALS

Over 100 Delicious Recipes for All-Time Favorite
Feel-Good Foods

KIM WILCOX

WITH CONTRIBUTIONS FROM

Frank Aloise
EXECUTIVE CHEF AT FOREST CREEK GOLF CLUB

Jen Bixby
MANAGER OF IT'S ALL SO YUMMY CAFÉ

Tee Dedrick
FOUNDER OF SPECIAL TEE COOKIES & CATERING

Brandon Frohne
WINNER OF COOKING CHANNEL'S *SNACK ATTACK*

Chris Grove
CERTIFIED FOOD JUDGE FOR THE WORLD FOOD
CHAMPIONSHIPS AND BBQ COOKBOOK AUTHOR

Dean Hitt
FOUNDER OF *TENNESSEE CUISINE* AND OWNER OF
TENNESSEE JACKS ON THE TOWN

Amy and Adam Kennedy and Chad Greenor
FOUNDERS AND OWNERS OF REFILL COFFEE CART

Kevin Moreland
OWNER OF MOMO'S RHYTHM AND RIBS ROADHOUSE GRILL

Lisa Varnado
FOUNDER OF MARBLE CITY SWEETS

Chris and Allyson Virden
FOUNDERS OF OLDE VIRDEN'S TENNESSEE PEPPER CO.

Wade Wilcox
OWNER OF IT'S ALL SO YUMMY CAFÉ

FOX CHAPEL
PUBLISHING

© 2023 by Kim Wilcox and Fox Chapel Publishing Company, Inc., 903 Square Street, Mount Joy, PA 17552.

Comfort Food Essentials is an original work, first published in 2023 by Fox Chapel Publishing Company, Inc. All rights reserved. No part of this publication may be reproduced, stored in a retrieval system or transmitted, in any form or by any means, electronic, mechanical, photocopying, recording or otherwise, without the prior written permission of the copyright holders.

Photography by Chris Grove. Food styling by the author and Chris Grove.

ISBN 978-1-4971-0320-7

Library of Congress Control Number: 2023938670

To learn more about the other great books from Fox Chapel Publishing, or to find a retailer near you, call toll-free 800-457-9112 or visit us at *www.FoxChapelPublishing.com*.

We are always looking for talented authors. To submit an idea, please send a brief inquiry to acquisitions@foxchapelpublishing.com.

Printed in China
First printing

Because working with cooking utensils, heat, and other materials inherently includes the risk of injury and damage, this book cannot guarantee that creating the recipes in this book is safe for everyone. For this reason, this book is sold without warranties or guarantees of any kind, expressed or implied, and the publisher and the author disclaim any liability for any injuries, losses, or damages caused in any way by the content of this book or the reader's use of the tools needed to complete the recipes presented here. The publisher and the author urge all readers to thoroughly review each recipe and to understand the use of all tools before beginning any recipe.

CONTENTS

Introduction

Decorating cookies is an annual family event. Someone was always the first and last one at the table: my daughter Sydney.

"Comfort food is the food that makes us feel good, satisfied, calm, cared for, and carefree. It's food that fills us up emotionally and physically. Finding comfort in food is a basic human experience."—Ellie Krieger

Comfort food is defined as "food prepared in a traditional style having a usually nostalgic or sentimental appeal." As I see it, it's not any specific food (although we all have our favorites). It's food that reminds you of good times. Food that soothes your soul and mends broken hearts. Foods that are like a big warm hug when you need it most. It's holiday gatherings, family tradition, and memories. Comfort food is any dish that truly makes you feel better. In this book, you'll find recipes for food to set the soul at ease, including some of the most popular comfort foods like mac and cheese (pages 94–96), spaghetti (page 77), chicken noodle soup (page 38), pizza (pages 92–93), meatloaf (page 79), lasagna (pages 60–61), homemade ice cream (pages 116–119), and so many more ranging from conventional favorites to unexpected delights.

My restaurant is known for tried-and-true comfort food and grilled cheese (perhaps the ultimate comfort food), but many of my warmest memories are related to foods cooked by my mom and grandmothers. It wasn't just the food they cooked; it was the comfort that it would bring us and the joy they had in making it for us. They would each add their own special touch to everything they prepared, whether it was my mom making sure we had dessert or grandma serving us in her threadbare apron.

The passing on of traditional family comfort food recipes is something that fills my heart with joy. It is important to me that my family have a record of our shared recipes and the

My granddaughter Halo's mom and dad both love to cook and she is always right there helping them.

My grandson Bentley loves to help us out at the café! Here he is helping me roll dog treats! (We cater to our guests' pets too!)

stories and memories tied to them. Almost all of these dishes have been prepared for me when I was young, and I've subsequently made them for my own kids and grandkids. Whether it's tweaking a family recipe in the restaurant and watching a customer savor that first delicious bite or teaching my grandkids to make the perfect cookies in my home kitchen, it's the love behind a meal that creates the best flavor.

My daughter Alley kissing a turkey! We have a family game we play where we dare each other to eat items left on the table. Alley won $5 for kissing the turkey!

Comfort food is about sharing with others. It's food that comes from the heart and spills out warmth and kindness to everyone who partakes. My hope is that you will enjoy these dishes as much as my family has!

—Kim

Sydney often talked Alley into pulling a chair up to the counter and joining her for a creative cooking afternoon!

Beautiful handwritten recipe cards add a special touch when cooking family favorites.

CHAPTER 1

Tools and Tips

T he cooking process, whether you're cooking as a family or simply preparing a meal to share, is part of the joy that makes something a comfort food in the first place! Your grandma's favorite rolling pin is just one of the secret ingredients to creating her signature pie crust, for example. The tools we use and the family tips and traditions we follow all combine to create the shared experiences and joys provided by comfort food favorites.

Cooking Utensils

If you peek into any cook's kitchen you are bound to find an assortment of their favorite tools of the trade. We all have those items that either make our adventure in the kitchen easier, more nostalgic, or both. For some it's the latest gadgets and gizmos, for others it's tools passed down through their family. Whatever you choose, it has to work for you and serve your culinary needs. A lot of my tools and décor were passed down from my family or are items that hold special memories for me. Here are a few of my favorite pieces to use.

Bundt Pans

Bundt pans were popularized in the 1950s and 1960s. Sadly, I don't think that a lot of people make Bundt cakes anymore. Because I love all things nostalgic, I use them for a few cakes and for some breads that I make. You will see in the cookbook how I used them for my pull-apart breads (see pages 32–33).

Cast Iron

My grandmother used cast iron to fry catfish, cook cornbread, and sauté okra. I use cast iron as much as I possibly can, as you will see in the recipes. I like the way well-seasoned cast iron cooks and how easy the cleanup is, and cast-iron cookware is very durable and has a nostalgic feel. I have a very large collection of cast iron that I am very proud of, and my children have already called dibs on it.

Spoon Rest

While spoon rests aren't necessary, this particular spoon rest is the one my grandmother kept on her stove. When I see it, it makes me smile and brings back the sweetest memories of her in the kitchen.

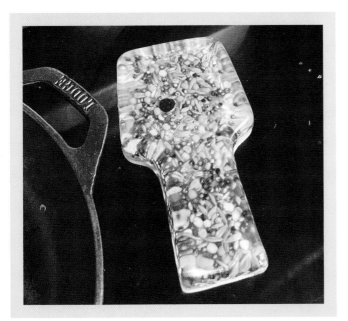

Mason Jars

They're not just for canning or pickling anymore! I use them all around my kitchen to store ingredients that I frequently use, colorful treats, cupcake wrappers, or toothpicks, to name only a few. I even use them as vases! It keeps things close by and I love the look of a mixed arrangement.

Hand Mixer

I think that every baker and cook aspires to own a countertop mixer. They are very handy, but never underestimate the hand mixer for smaller jobs. It is perfect for small-batch whipped cream, beating egg whites, or shredding.

Recipe Box

I keep most of my recipes in several binders full of plastic sleeves, but my absolute favorite, most frequently used recipes are in this box on my counter. I always know just where they are whenever I need them.

Chalkboard

Years ago, I painted a wall in my kitchen with chalkboard paint to help me keep track of my busy schedule. I've used it for grocery lists, recipes, and, if I've had to do a large quantity of baking, I've used hash marks on there to help me keep track. It's also a great place to write a dinner request or sweet note.

Wooden Spoons

My mother had a wooden spoon collection that she displayed on the wall of the kitchen when I was growing up. They were beautiful but we weren't allowed to use them. When I started cooking, I tried every shape and size until I found the ones that worked best for me. I like to use wooden spoons that are strong and durable for getting the job done and I love a flat-edged spoon for scraping because it won't scratch pots and pans. With a little care and hand washing, your wooden spoons should last forever and become a great family heirloom.

Tea Towels

I love a good cotton tea towel, and I find myself reaching for one all the time in the kitchen. I love the large size and how absorbent they are. If I am steaming spinach, I use a tea towel to squeeze the water out of the spinach. If I am steeping lavender for lemonade, I use a tea towel to strain the lavender out of the simple syrup. I do have some decorative tea towels, but I have a drawer full of large white tea towels.

Bowls and Dessert Cups

I am not of the mindset that everything must match; that's just my style. I believe that when presenting salads or soups or desserts, the presentation should be fun and interesting. I often look at garage sales and thrift stores for new and interesting pieces to use. By using different sizes, shapes, and heights, you create visual stimulation for those enjoying the meal and a lovely display for your food.

Making Substitutions

Since everyone has a different childhood, cultural background, and upbringing, comfort food looks different for us all. Anything easy to make and easily passed down through generations qualifies as delicious comfort food. These recipes include the flavors and reference the brands that many of my friends and family love, but feel free to replace them with your own favorites or add in beloved ingredients! Does your nephew prefer shell-shaped pasta to elbow macaroni? Go with shells! Is your grandmother a long-time fan of olives mixed into her egg salad? Throw in some chopped olives! Many people find comfort in the flavor of a specific brand of ketchup or cola. It's comfort food, so go with what is most comfortable!

Comfort food can also have a lot of calories, fats, salt, and sugar, so sometimes you might want to make healthier substitutions. You can always make small changes to lighten up your favorite recipes while not missing out on the satisfaction of a classic meal. Here are a just a handful of smart tricks that help to bump up the nutrition level of your favorite comfort meals:

- **Try using multigrain or whole wheat pasta instead of enriched pasta.**
- **Try mixing extra vegetables into your mac and cheese or soups to add flavor and fiber.**
- **You can replace half the oil in cake recipes with applesauce!**
- **Greek yogurt can work as an alternative to sour cream.**
- **Using fresh herbs in place of salt-based blends is an easy way to cut sodium.**
- **Play around with starches—swap sweet potatoes for regular potatoes.**
- **Try different proteins! Turkey bacon is a great option, for example.**

Time-Honored Cooking Tips

Remember, cooking (especially cooking these comforting family favorites) should be fun and not full of stress. Be open to experimentation, and do not be afraid to try new ingredients. I've picked up a few tips and tricks over the years from friends and family that will help make preparing these dishes as warm and rewarding an experience as sharing them with your loved ones. Here are a few of my favorites:

- To keep baked goods soft, store them in an airtight container with a slice of store-bought bread.
- Need butter for a recipe, but yours is too hard? Soften your butter by putting it in a zippered plastic bag and letting the bag sit in warm water for a few minutes.
- Wrapping a damp paper towel around lettuce and other produce keeps it fresh!
- Sprinkle baking soda on the bottom of burnt pans to clean them with ease.
- Keep berries in glass jars rather than the plastic containers from the store to help them last longer.
- Peel onions under running water to prevent the fumes from making you cry.
- To see if the eggs you're using are spoiled or not, place them in a cup or bowl of water: fresh eggs will sink and spoiled eggs will float.
- Sprinkle flour on bacon before baking to make it extra-crispy.
- Soak potatoes in cold water before peeling to loosen the skin. This makes it so easy to peel!
- When using oil to fry something, use a wooden spoon to check to see if it's hot enough. Bubbles around the spoon mean yes.
- Use rinds and ends of cheese in mac and cheese instead of throwing them away.
- Spray your measuring spoons and cups with nonstick spray before measuring sticky liquids like honey or syrup.
- Use a lint roller to easily clean up items like spilled sprinkles.
- Make your own nonstick cooking spray by mixing 1 part oil with 5 parts water in a spray bottle.
- Ripen and soften bananas in a pinch by baking them for 5 to 7 minutes in an oven set to 350°F.

I've sprinkled a few more tips and tricks throughout the book that are specific to each recipe. Remember to read through the included Notes before you begin cooking to see if you can make your life easier or substitute one of your favorite flavors!

CHAPTER 2

Breakfast Favorites

We call breakfast the most important meal for a reason—not only does it provide the energy we need to kick-start our day, it also provides an opportunity to create priceless memories. My daughters may no longer sit with ponytails and giggles waiting for their banana pancakes, but those joyful moments last forever.

page 16

page 15

page 14

page 18

page 19

Sausage Gravy

Makes 6–8 servings

I was a firm believer that gravy belonged only on mashed potatoes and not on my breakfast biscuits until I had my first plate of biscuits and sausage gravy at a truck stop in Ottumwa, Iowa. I have been obsessed since that day! I became a self-titled "gravy snob" and set out to make the perfect sausage gravy. This, my friends, is my version of the ultimate sausage gravy!

Ingredients

- 1 lb. sage sausage (or use plain if desired)
- ¾–1 cup flour
- ½ gallon whole milk
- Salt and pepper to taste
- 1 tsp. poultry seasoning, optional

Instructions

1. Put your sausage in a preheated cast-iron skillet on medium heat and cook until it is brown and there is no pink. Break up as many of the large chunks as you can.
2. Add a sprinkle of salt and pepper and the poultry seasoning. Stir to incorporate.
3. Turn the heat down to medium, add the flour, and stir well to coat all the sausage. You may have to add a little extra flour if you think the gravy looks too thin.
4. Slowly stir in the milk and let it come to a slow boil. Taste and adjust the seasonings as necessary. I like mine very peppery.
5. Cook until the gravy starts to get thick. Note that your gravy will thicken as it cools.
6. Pour generously over your favorite prepared-from-scratch or frozen biscuits and serve.

Notes

Adjust the flavor of your gravy by using different sausage flavors.

Make your gravy thinner by adding more milk.

When making your biscuits, add a pat of butter to the top of each biscuit prior to baking!

Biscuits and gravy is a breakfast staple in the Midwest and South.

Big Orange Stack

Makes 4 servings

We were playing with food again, trying to produce a unique breakfast idea at the café for an event that we were catering. I wanted to present a breakfast dish that would be unique, visually appealing, and stick to your ribs for a while. We played with flavors, elements, sauces, and textures before we finally decided on this combination. Enjoy!

Ingredients

- 4 buttermilk biscuits, buttered and split
- 2 ripe tomatoes, cut into slices
- 12 slices crispy bacon
- Equal parts sriracha and orange marmalade (see step 1 below)
- 4 eggs
- 2 cups shredded cheese
- Sliced avocado
- Salt and pepper to taste

Instructions

1. In a small bowl, mix equal parts of sriracha and orange marmalade, set aside.
2. On each plate, place a split biscuit or slice of cornbread.
3. On top of the bread, lay two slices of tomato, salted and peppered.
4. Lay 3 slices of warm bacon on each serving and top with about ⅓ cup of shredded cheese. Let the warm bacon melt the cheese.
5. Take a teaspoon and drizzle the sriracha-orange sauce over the bacon and cheese.
6. Cook the eggs sunny-side up and gently place them on each stack. Drizzle the remaining sriracha-orange sauce over each one.
7. Garnish with fresh cracked pepper and avocado slices.

Notes

This is a great game-day breakfast, easy to make at your tailgate.

Instead of buttermilk biscuits, try using 4 pieces of warm Country Cornbread (page 28), Mexican Cornbread (page 30), or Cranberry Cornbread (page 31).

Extra sriracha-orange sauce is great on wings, as a dip for chicken tenders, or on fish.

Experiment with the type of cheese you use. Any smoked cheese, pepper jack, or soft extra-melty cheeses would be good.

Banana Pancakes

Makes 3 servings

My first time trying banana pancakes was on vacation in Mexico. We ventured out early one morning and found the cutest little locally owned café. Banana pancakes just so happened to be on their special board that morning. They ended up being the most delicious, moist pancakes I've ever had. I think you will find these pancakes very a-peeling!

Ingredients

- 2 cups baking mix, I use Bisquick
- 1 cup whole milk
- 2 eggs
- 1 tsp. vanilla
- 2 Tbsp. melted butter
- 2 mashed ripe bananas

Instructions

1. Preheat a lightly oiled griddle to 375°F.
2. In a medium bowl, stir together by hand everything but the bananas until well mixed.
3. Add the bananas in and mix gently.
4. Pour about ¼ cup of the batter onto the hot griddle, leaving space between the pancakes.
5. Cook until the pancakes are brown on the edges and there are bubbles coming through to the top. Flip and cook for another 2 minutes or until golden brown.
6. Remove and serve with warm maple syrup.

Notes

Garnish your pancakes with whipped cream, caramelized bananas, or caramel sauce.

Make an extra batch and freeze them for future use. Freeze in a single layer in storage bags, then warm them up in the morning!

Did you know that a cluster of bananas is called a hand and consists of 10–20 bananas, which are known as fingers?

Upside-Down Pineapple Pancakes
Makes 3 servings

Pancakes make us dream of lazy weekend mornings in our pajamas with a hot cup of coffee. These upside-down pineapple pancakes are a decadent but minimal-effort way to start your weekend. They will have you asking yourself: is this dessert or is this breakfast?

Ingredients
- 2 cups baking mix, I use Bisquick
- ¾ cup whole milk
- One 20-oz. can drained, sliced pineapple rings, reserve ¼ cup pineapple juice
- 2 eggs
- 2½ Tbsp. sugar
- 1 tsp. vanilla
- 2 Tbsp. melted butter
- Maraschino cherries, drained, stems removed

Instructions
1. Preheat a lightly oiled griddle to 375°F.
2. In a medium bowl, stir together by hand everything but the pineapple rings and cherries, until well mixed.
3. Place a pineapple ring on the griddle and put a cherry in the center hole. Repeat with about 4–5 rings and cherries.
4. Pour ⅓–½ cup of batter on top of the pineapple rings.
5. Cook until the pancakes are brown on the edges and there are bubbles coming through to the top. Flip and cook for another 2 minutes or until golden brown.
6. Remove and serve with warm maple syrup and a pat of butter.

Notes
Pineapples take 18–20 months to become ripe enough to harvest.

To make these into a dessert, layer them with a mascarpone and pineapple mixture and serve with whipped cream and a cherry.

Use any pancake mix recipe that you wish—including your family's secret recipe! The one I use is tried and true for me.

Chocolate Chip Pancakes

Makes 3 servings

I loved making these for my kids when they were growing up. The melted chocolate chips created such a warm and comforting aroma in the morning. The girls thought that having chocolate for breakfast was really getting away with something, little did they know it was just my way of loving them.

Ingredients

- 2 cups baking mix, I use Bisquick
- 1 cup whole milk
- 2 eggs
- 2½ Tbsp. sugar
- 2 Tbsp. melted butter
- 1 cup chocolate chips, whatever variety you like best

Instructions

1. Preheat a lightly oiled griddle to 375°F.
2. In a medium bowl, stir together by hand everything but the chocolate chips, until well mixed.
3. Add the chocolate chips in and mix gently.
4. Pour about ¼ cup of the batter onto the hot griddle, leaving space between the pancakes.
5. Cook until the pancakes are brown on the edges and there are bubbles coming through to the top. Flip and cook for another 2 minutes or until golden brown.
6. Remove and serve with warm maple syrup and a pat of butter.

Notes

Vary the flavor of chips you use according to what you and your family enjoy most. For fun, try a mix of milk chocolate, dark chocolate, and semi-sweet chips.

These pancakes freeze well and make a great after-school or late-night snack served with a scoop of ice cream on top.

Fun and delicious garnishes include whipped cream, chocolate syrup, and chocolate chips or shavings.

Stuffed French Toast
Makes 6 servings

The morning after slumber parties we always made French toast. The only stuffing we did back then was into our hungry mouths! This stuffed French toast has all the elements of the classic with a hint of "I'm so fancy."

Ingredients

- 8-oz. block cream cheese, room temperature
- ½ cup powdered sugar
- 1 Tbsp. vanilla
- 3 Tbsp. raspberry preserves
- 12 slices thick brioche bread
- 1 cup whole milk
- 3 eggs, beaten
- 1 tsp. sugar

Instructions

1. In a small mixing bowl, beat together the cream cheese, powdered sugar, and vanilla until it is smooth and spreadable.
2. Stir in the raspberry preserves.
3. Preheat a lightly oiled griddle to 375°F.
4. Take a piece of bread and spread a generous amount of the cream cheese filling on it. Top it with another piece of bread so it looks like a sandwich.
5. Do this until you have used all the bread.
6. In a small bowl, whisk the milk, eggs, and sugar until well mixed. Dip your brioche sandwiches in there, making sure you coat them completely.
7. Put a little butter on your griddle and cook until golden brown on each side.
8. Remove and serve with butter, syrup, and fresh fruit.

Notes

Dust your French toast with powdered sugar or even raw sugar for added texture.

Use any fruit preserve in this recipe that you like. Orange marmalade is also very tasty!

Did you know that French toast is also known as "eggy bread" and "German toast"?

November 28 is National French Toast Day—mark your calendars!

Baked Eggs Napoleon

Chef Chris Grove, Certified Food Judge for the World Food Championships and BBQ Cookbook Author

Makes 4 servings

Named for Napoleon Dynamite of movie fame rather than Bonaparte ... as in, "Napoleon, give me some of your tots." One morning, I had leftover tater tots and came up with this creation, which has become the most popular and most frequently copied recipe on Nibble Me This (nibblemethis.com).

Ingredients

- 60 crispy tater tots, cooked according to package directions
- 1–2 Tbsp. butter or bacon fat
- ½ cup diced sweet onion
- ¼ cup diced red bell pepper
- 1 Tbsp. cooking oil
- 4 oz. breakfast sausage, browned
- 2 oz. mozzarella, shredded
- 4 large eggs
- ¾ tsp. fajita seasoning, divided
- 2 green onions, sliced

Instructions

1. Preheat a cast-iron skillet over medium-high heat and add the butter or bacon fat. Add the onion and bell pepper, season with ½ teaspoon of the fajita seasoning, then sauté until tender and turning translucent, about 5 minutes. Remove from the heat.

2. Break the tater tots in half and place them in a large bowl. Mix them with the onion, bell pepper, and sausage.

3. Dampen a paper towel with cooking oil and wipe the insides of 4 small ramekins (about a 3" diameter). Divide the tot mixture between the 4 ramekins and use a large spoon to press each down, leaving a slight depression or divot in the middle. Top with the mozzarella cheese and break an egg on top of each ramekin. Lightly season the eggs with the remaining ¼ teaspoon of fajita seasoning.

4. Preheat an oven or indirect grill to 400°F. Place the ramekins in the center of the oven or grill and cook until the egg whites turn white and set up, about 20–30 minutes.

5. Remove the ramekins from the heat. They may be served in the ramekins with a fork but warn your guests that the dishes are hot. We prefer to use a silicone spatula to pry the Eggs Napoleon from the ramekins onto a plate, garnishing each with green onion.

CHAPTER 3

Sweet and Savory Breads

Over the past few years, it seems like everyone realized the comfort that could be found in homemade bread. There's just nothing quite like it, and there is as much joy in making it as there is in eating it. As a foodie, I consider a fresh loaf of homemade bread to be man's best friend.

page 24

page 31

page 26

page 28

page 27

Beer Bread

Makes one loaf

Beer bread is easy to prepare and has long been at the center of the table for family gatherings. If we're having a family meal, there is guaranteed to be beer bread hanging around. This is a basic bread recipe that is delicious as is, but it's also easy to customize with the addition of simple ingredients. You can make a triple batch and season each loaf individually to create three varieties.

Ingredients

- 3 cups self-rising flour
- 2 Tbsp. sugar
- 12 oz. full-bodied beer
- Homemade butter of choice (see page 25) or Honey Butter (see page 25), for serving

Instructions

1. Preheat oven to 350°F.
2. Open the beer and pour it into a large mixing bowl, stir and let it sit until there are no more bubbles.
3. In a medium mixing bowl, combine flour and sugar, mix well.
4. Stir in the beer and mix until the ingredients are incorporated.
5. Put the mixture in a greased loaf pan and bake for 35 minutes.
6. Cool on a wire rack.

Notes

While your loaf cools, drizzle it with olive oil or melted butter and add a sprinkling of coarse sea salt.

Using a stronger beer will yield tastier results.

Homemade Butter

Makes 1 cup butter

Y'all, I'm not shy about my love of butter, and this recipe takes my obsession to another level. I remember showing my kids and employees how we could make our own butter in a matter of minutes at home, no churn and wooden stool needed. They were mesmerized by the quick process and how creamy and delicious the result was.

Instructions

1. Add the heavy cream to a chilled mixing bowl or a chilled stand mixer bowl.
2. Start mixing on low, then increase the speed as the cream starts to thicken.
3. Add the salt.
4. As you are mixing, the cream will turn into whipped cream. Keep mixing.
5. The mixture will separate into a liquid and a solid.
6. Over a strainer, strain off the liquid. This is buttermilk, which you can keep and use as needed.
7. Rinse your butter solid with cold water.
8. Now is the time in which you can add flavors and make a compound butter, if desired (I've listed a few of my favorite flavors in the Notes).
9. Roll your butter into a large ball, wrap it in plastic wrap, and refrigerate.

Ingredients

- 2 cups chilled heavy cream
- 1 tsp. salt

Notes

To create unsalted butter, eliminate the salt.

Save the milk residue from the bowl and use it in soups and in baking.

Here are a few of my favorite butter flavors: orange zest and finely diced dried cranberries, blue cheese, Italian herbs, honey or hot honey, rosemary, diced pickled onions and jalapeños.

Honey Butter

Makes 1 cup

When I was young, my mom was known for mixing up a big batch of honey butter for the family. I've enjoyed sharing her recipe with my kids and grandkids—it's become a family favorite. We also serve it at the café with our cornbread. I think it's the combination of sweet and savory combined with great memories that I love so much.

Instructions

1. Put your butter in a mixing bowl and beat it until it is creamy and fluffy.
2. Add the honey and mix until it's smooth.
3. Store in the refrigerator.

Ingredients

- 2 sticks butter, room temperature
- ⅓ cup honey

Notes

If you like a little kick, use hot honey instead of plain honey.

For another flavor twist, add a little cinnamon.

This is great on cornbread, toast, peanut butter sandwiches, biscuits, and fried chicken.

Momma's Lemon Bread

Makes 8 servings

This is a lemon bread that my mom made for us only on special occasions. When she gave this recipe to me, she included these words: "Cut in thin slices when it gets cold. NO butter is needed, good with coffee or anytime. YUMMMM, enjoy." I added the candied lemon peels because they are beautiful, a little fancy, and add an additional layer of zest.

Ingredients

- 1½ cups sugar, divided
- ⅓ cup shortening, melted
- 3 tsp. pure lemon extract
- 2 eggs
- 1½ cups flour
- 1½ tsp. baking powder
- 1 tsp. salt
- ½ cup milk
- 1 lemon rind, grated
- ½ cup chopped walnuts, optional
- Juice of 1 lemon
- Candied lemon peels

Instructions

1. Preheat the oven to 350°F and grease your loaf pan.
2. In a large bowl, mix 1 cup of the sugar, the shortening, and the lemon extract.
3. To that add eggs, flour, baking powder, and salt, alternating with the milk.
4. Stir in the lemon rind and chopped nuts.
5. Pour into your loaf pan and bake for one hour or until a toothpick comes out clean.
6. While your loaf is baking, dissolve ½ cup of the sugar in the lemon juice.
7. When your bread is done and still warm, poke holes in the top of the bread with a fork and pour the lemon juice mixture over the bread, letting it dribble into the holes.
8. When cool, add candied lemon peels.

Notes

The toothpick test allows us to know when our cakes and breads are done so that when we slice them, they'll hold together. It helps us know that no excessive moisture is left in baked items.

If you want to vary this recipe a bit, try adding fresh rosemary, blueberries, or poppy seeds.

Super Moist Banana Bread

Makes one loaf

If you hang around me long enough, you might hear me say, "Don't throw away those soft bananas, I need them!" Open my freezer and you will find overripe bananas just waiting to be part of this moist and delicious treat. This bread is no-doubt irresistible right out of the oven, but it also freezes well. You may just want to double this recipe!

Ingredients

- 1¾ cups all-purpose flour
- ⅔ cup granulated sugar
- 2 tsp. baking powder
- ½ tsp. kosher salt
- 2 eggs, room temperature, beaten well
- ¼ cup whole milk
- ¼ cup vegetable oil
- 1½ cups mashed, overripe bananas
- ½ tsp. vanilla
- Chopped nuts, optional

Notes

Do not throw out your brown bananas, they make the best bread! Make sure you peel them before you freeze them in freezer bags.

You can also drizzle this loaf with a cream cheese glaze while the bread is still warm.

This bread pairs well with coffee!

Instructions

1. Preheat oven to 350°F.
2. In a large mixing bowl, mix the flour, sugar, baking powder, and salt.
3. In a medium bowl, mix the eggs, bananas, and oil until they are fully incorporated.
4. Add the vanilla and mix.
5. Add the dry ingredients to the banana mixture and stir well. Add the nuts if desired.
6. Pour into a greased loaf pan and bake for 1 hour.
7. Cool on a wire rack.

Country Cornbread
Makes 8–12 servings

My family loves cornbread and we tend to enjoy it a little on the sweet side, which is not always a popular opinion. You can use this recipe and omit the sugar if your family gravitates more toward savory. Either way, it's a delightfully flavorful and moist cornbread.

Ingredients
- 2½ cups self-rising yellow cornmeal
- 2 cups buttermilk
- ⅓ cup melted shortening, I use Crisco
- 2 eggs, beaten
- ¼ cup sugar
- 1½ tsp. kosher salt
- One 15.25-oz. can corn, partially drained

Instructions
1. Preheat the oven to 350°F.
2. Grease a 9" x 13" pan, use cupcake liners in a cupcake pan, or lightly grease a cast-iron skillet.
3. Mix all the ingredients together in a bowl and stir gently to incorporate.
4. Bake for 20–25 minutes or until golden brown. Serve hot.

Notes
This cornbread is great topped with butter, honey, honey butter, or jam.

For a nice flavor variation, substitute a small can of chopped green chilies for the corn.

For a real treat, put a few tablespoons of pimento cheese on top of the bread and broil it for a few minutes until the cheese is soft and melting.

Mexican Cornbread

Makes 8–12 servings

Yes, I love cornbread (hence all the cornbread recipes I've included), and for those of you who know me, you know I also love spicy food! This cornbread has a nice kick to it. It is perfect with a steamy bowl of pinto beans, with a scoop of pimento cheese on top, or for breakfast with eggs and bacon.

Ingredients

- ¼ cup chopped yellow onion
- ¼ cup chopped green pepper
- ¼ cup diced jalapeño, fresh or pickled
- 2 eggs
- ½ cup sour cream
- 1¼ cups buttermilk
- One 15.25-oz. can corn
- ½ Tbsp. hot sauce or salsa
- 2¼ cups self-rising yellow cornmeal
- 2 Tbsp. sugar
- 1 tsp. kosher salt
- ¼ tsp. cayenne pepper

Instructions

1. Preheat oven to 350°F.
2. Grease a 9" x 13" pan, use cupcake liners in a cupcake pan, or lightly grease a cast-iron skillet.
3. Mix the wet ingredients together in a large bowl and set aside.
4. Combine the dry ingredients together and stir into the wet ingredients.
5. Pour into the prepared baking vessel and bake for 15–20 minutes until lightly browned. Serve warm.

Notes

Serve with soups, stews, pinto beans, or as a side dish.

Try adding a scoop of pimento cheese on top and placing it under the broiler for a few minutes to melt the cheese.

This recipe works great as a crust for a Mexican casserole.

For a flavor variation, try adding black olives, lime zest, or cilantro.

Cranberry Cornbread
Makes 8–12 servings

I experimented with this recipe around Thanksgiving one year. We always have cornbread for holiday dinners, but I pondered how to add some holiday flair to this family favorite. The tartness of the cranberries and the bright orange zest bring a hint of holiday to the cornbread. I absolutely love the result!

Ingredients
- 2½ cups self-rising yellow cornmeal
- 2 cups buttermilk
- ⅓ cup melted shortening, I use Crisco
- 2 eggs, beaten
- ¼ cup sugar
- 1½ tsp. kosher salt
- 1 cup dried cranberries or craisins
- 1 Tbsp. orange zest

Instructions
1. Preheat the oven to 350°F.
2. Grease a 9" x 13" pan, use cupcake liners in a cupcake pan, or lightly grease a cast-iron skillet.
3. Mix all the ingredients together in a bowl and stir gently to incorporate.
4. Bake for 20–25 minutes or until golden brown. Serve hot.

Notes
Serve with an orange zest compound butter: mix 2 sticks of room-temperature butter with 1 Tbsp. of fresh orange zest.

Cornbread can be baked or fried and it's known by many names, including Johnny cakes, corn pone, and hush puppies.

If you want to shake things up a bit, add chopped almonds to your batter before baking.

Savory Pull-Apart Bread

Makes 10 servings

This bread is stunning, remarkably like monkey bread but made with savory spices. Customize the seasonings you use to complement what you are serving it with. It is fun to make and even more fun to eat—a definite showstopper on the table!

Ingredients

- 1 package frozen buttermilk biscuits, I use a Pillsbury Grands! 20-biscuit package
- 2 sticks butter
- Various herbs, such as poppy seeds, toasted white sesame seeds, black sesame seeds, parsley, granulated garlic, smoked paprika, sea salt, basil, and rosemary
- Olive oil and Italian seasoning, for dipping

Instructions

1. Preheat the oven to 350°F and grease a Bundt cake pan.
2. Let the biscuits come to room temperature and cut them into quarters.
3. Melt the butter in a shallow bowl and set aside.
4. Put each herb on an individual small bowl or plate.
5. Dip each biscuit piece into butter and roll it in one of the herbs. Place it in the cake pan.
6. Continue with each biscuit piece, using different herbs and placing them on top of one another in the pan.
7. When all the biscuits are coated and placed in the pan, pour the remaining butter over the top.
8. Bake for 45–50 minutes until the biscuits are done. Cool for 15 minutes before turning the bread onto a serving platter.
9. Serve warm with a plate of olive oil and Italian seasoning for dipping.

Notes

You can use tubes of refrigerated biscuits, as well. You will need 4–6 tubes.

This is a beautiful addition to your dinner table. Try to use various colored herbs for the most spectacular presentation.

Compound butters make a great side for this bread.

Spiced Rum Fruitcake Pull-Apart Bread

Makes 8–10 servings

I was out running those last-minute Christmas errands when what to my wondering eyes should appear, but fruitcake. These colorful, cellophane-wrapped fruitcakes that sit patiently on the counter by the cash register every Christmas while people poke, prod, and laugh. I looked at it and thought, what can we do to make sure fruitcake doesn't get a bad rap anymore? I'm here for you, fruitcake!

Ingredients

- 1 cup dark or spiced rum
- ½ cup chopped dried apricots
- ½ cup raisins
- ½ cup craisins
- 1 cup chopped dried apples
- ½ cup chopped dried dates
- 1 tsp. orange zest
- 1 cup toasted, chopped pecans
- 1 package frozen buttermilk biscuits, I use a Pillsbury Grands! 20-biscuit package
- 2–3 sticks butter
- 1 cup sugar
- 1 tsp. cinnamon

Instructions

1. Put the rum in a saucepan and heat for 3 minutes on medium, until warm.
2. Add the dried fruit and orange zest to the rum, put the mixture in a bowl and refrigerate it for 24 hours to allow the rum to soak into the fruit.
3. Preheat the oven to 350°F and generously grease a Bundt cake pan.
4. Let the biscuits come to room temperature, then cut them into quarters.
5. Take the fruit mixture out and set it aside.
6. Melt the butter in a bowl, then mix the sugar and cinnamon in another bowl.
7. Drop each biscuit piece into the butter, then roll it in the cinnamon-sugar mixture.
8. Place the biscuits in a layer in the Bundt pan. When you have one layer done, add spoonsful of the fruit mixture and a few of the nuts, then continue to layer biscuits and the fruit mixture until the pan is about 1" below full.
9. Combine the remaining juice from the fruit and rum mixture, butter, and cinnamon-sugar and mix well. Pour this over the unbaked biscuits.
10. Put the pan on a baking sheet and bake for 50 minutes.
11. Cool on a rack before inverting it onto a serving dish.

Notes

Use a combination of the fruit and nuts that you most enjoy.

This is best served warm!

CHAPTER 4

Satisfying Soups

Some of my most vivid childhood memories revolve around soup—especially my mom's go-to cold remedy of hot chicken broth. Today I prefer a thick, creamy soup loaded with warm, comforting flavors and ingredients—and our customers definitely agree!

page 37

page 44

page 36

page 45

page 39

Roasted Carrot and Sweet Onion Soup

Makes 8 servings

This soup is visually stunning and looks as if it took you all day to prepare. The truth is that it's quite easy, but you don't have to share that secret! The carrot and onion combination lend a slightly sweet and mildly savory flavor to this comforting soup.

Ingredients

- 2 lbs. carrots, peeled and sliced into chunks
- 2 sweet yellow onions, peeled and quartered
- 2 cloves of garlic, peeled
- 3–4 Tbsp. olive oil
- Salt and pepper
- 8 cups chicken or vegetable stock
- 2 cups heavy cream
- 1 cup sour cream
- 3 Tbsp. pickled jalapeño juice
- Fresh coarse cracked black pepper
- Green onions, chopped

Instructions

1. Preheat the oven to 375°F.
2. Line a sheet pan with parchment paper and spread the carrots, onions, and garlic evenly on the pan.
3. Drizzle the vegetables with olive oil and season with salt and pepper. Toss them with your hands until everything is coated.
4. Roast the vegetables in the oven for 35–45 minutes, until everything is tender.
5. Add the stock to a large stockpot and bring it to a low boil. Add the vegetables and let them simmer for 20 minutes.
6. Using an immersion blender, blend the soup until it is smooth.
7. Add the heavy cream, ¼ cup at a time. If your soup is too thick, add more stock.
8. In a small bowl, mix the sour cream and jalapeño juice.
9. To serve, garnish the soup with a swirl of the sour cream, black pepper, and green onion.

Notes

Use plain sour cream if you don't care for jalapeño juice.

Spice up your soup if you'd like by adding spicy seasoning to the vegetables while they are roasting. I like to use Olde Virden's Spice Blends—my favorite for this dish is Red Hot.

Oven-Roasted Garlic and Cauliflower Soup

Makes 8 servings

I had requests at the café for cauliflower soup. I had honestly never made it and was not sure about the process, let alone the result! When a local farmer generously gifted us a box of fresh cauliflower, there was no better time to make this soup. It was delicious! What a gift our local farmers are.

Ingredients

- 2 large heads cauliflower
- 2 large white onions, chopped
- 7 garlic cloves, chopped
- 4 Tbsp. olive oil
- 8 cups chicken stock
- Salt and pepper
- 2 tsp. cumin
- Crispy bacon, crumbled
- Green onions, chopped
- French's fried crispy jalapeños

Instructions

1. Preheat the oven to 450°F. Line a baking pan with parchment paper.
2. Prepare the cauliflower by cutting it into small pieces, being careful to remove the stems. Lay the cauliflower on the baking sheet and add the onions and garlic.
3. Drizzle the vegetables with olive oil and use your hands to mix, making sure all the pieces are coated. Season with salt, pepper, and cumin.
4. Place the baking sheet in the oven and roast for 30 minutes or until the edges of the cauliflower are golden brown.
5. Remove from the oven and set aside a few pieces of the cauliflower for garnish.
6. Put the cauliflower, onions, and garlic into your blender. Add the chicken stock and blend until smooth. You may have to do this in 2 to 3 batches.
7. You can control how thick or thin your soup is with the amount of stock you add. You can also blend it smooth or leave a few small chunks if you like more texture.
8. To serve your soup, place it in bowl and use the set-aside cauliflower, bacon, green onions, and crispy jalapeños for garnish.

Notes

If you prefer a vegetarian soup, opt for vegetable broth in place of the chicken stock and eliminate the bacon garnish.

Cauliflower is a major source of vitamins C and K, and vitamin B6.

Cauliflower is versatile and nutritious! It can be eaten raw, fried, boiled, mashed, steamed, grilled, roasted, or pickled. It takes well to a variety of your favorite seasonings.

When blending hot soup, remove the center cap from the lid, fill your blender halfway and place a towel over the top of the blender lid.

Creamy Chicken Noodle Soup

Makes 6 servings

This soup provides a bowl of hot comfort when you need it most. Don't wait until you're sick to enjoy this soup, your family will jump up and down when they know it's what's for dinner! Fill mason jars and share with your friends, they will thank you!

Ingredients

- 2 lbs. chicken breasts, baked and shredded
- 3 cups egg noodles, I use Country Pasta Homemade Egg Noodles
- 2 Tbsp. vegetable or olive oil
- 1 large yellow onion, diced
- 4 carrots, chopped
- 3 celery stalks, chopped
- 3 garlic cloves, minced
- 5 cups chicken broth
- 3 Tbsp. chopped fresh parsley
- 2 bay leaves
- ¼ tsp. cayenne pepper
- Salt and pepper, to taste
- ½ cup heavy cream
- 2½ cups whole or 2% milk
- ¼ cup butter
- ¼ cup plus 3 Tbsp. flour

Notes

Baking and shredding your chicken can be super simple. Season it with salt, pepper, granulated garlic, and dried parsley. Bake covered in a dish at 350°F until the internal temperature reaches 165°F. Remove from the oven and let it sit for about 15 minutes. Cut the breasts into quarters and place them in the bowl of a stand mixer, then use your paddle attachment to shred the chicken.

Because of the higher fat content in whole milk, I use it in this soup to create a creamier texture.

I always use Country Pasta Homemade Style Egg Pasta in my noodle soups because it holds up well, the texture is perfect, and, in this soup, each noodle tastes like a big warm hug.

Instructions

1. In a large pot, heat the oil on medium heat and add the onion, carrots, and celery. Sauté until tender. Add the garlic and cook for 1 minute longer.
2. Add the chicken broth, bay leaves, cayenne pepper, and parsley. Let it come to a boil.
3. Add the shredded chicken and the noodles. Boil until the noodles are tender.
4. Reduce the heat to a simmer and remove the bay leaves.
5. Melt the butter in a medium saucepan on medium heat. Add the flour and stir for 2 minutes until well mixed. Slowly add the milk and whisk to make sure there are no lumps.
6. Whisk in the cream and bring to a boil.
7. Add the milk mixture to the chicken soup and mix well.

Christmas Eve Chili

Makes 8 servings

This is my family's traditional meal before the much-anticipated opening of gifts. My mom always made it for us on Christmas Eve and I have carried that tradition on for 38 years. I am a beans-in-my-chili kind of gal, and I use at least three types of beans. Use whatever you like best in yours. The same goes for seasonings. You'll notice I use French's Chili-O seasoning. It's what my mom used, and I continue to use it, too, because it is what my family loves. There was one Christmas when I used my own mix—the next morning my stocking was full of coal!

Ingredients

- 2½ lbs. ground beef
- 2 cups diced onions
- 12 Tbsp. preferred seasoning, I use French's Chili-O seasoning
- 2½ Tbsp. brown sugar
- One 46-oz. can tomato juice
- One 28-oz. can crushed tomatoes
- One 28-oz. can diced tomatoes
- One 28-oz. can tomatoes and green chiles
- Two 15-oz. cans dark red kidney beans, drained
- Two 15-oz. cans black beans, drained
- Three 15-oz. cans chili beans, undrained
- Salt and pepper to taste

Instructions

1. In a large stock pot on medium-high heat, brown the ground beef and onions. When the beef is brown, drain the fat.
2. Add the seasoning mix and stir well to incorporate.
3. Add the remaining ingredients and mix well. Bring to a boil then turn to low and simmer all day if you can, stirring every hour or so.
4. Serve piping hot with whatever fixings you enjoy!

Notes

If you have extra chili, you can freeze it in smaller containers and use it for chili dogs, nachos, or for a quick meal when you do not feel like cooking!

Our family loves to make chili pies. We set up a buffet of corn chips, shredded cheese, diced onions, olives, jalapeños, and sour cream and let everyone make their own.

Buffalo Chicken Chili

Makes approximately 10 servings

This chili recipe was inspired by my love of spicy foods and warm, comforting bowls of chili. It has the flavor of hot wings that we crave, without the messy fingers.

Ingredients

- 2 Tbsp. olive oil
- 2 Tbsp. butter
- 5 garlic cloves, minced
- 6 celery stalks with leaves, diced
- 2 cups diced onions
- 2 cups chopped carrots
- Two 15-oz. cans pinto beans, drained
- Two 15-oz. cans black beans, drained
- One 28-oz. can crushed tomatoes
- One 28-oz. can tomatoes with green chiles
- Two 16-oz. bottles beer
- 3 cups chicken stock
- 1½ cups hot sauce
- 3 tsp. cumin
- 3 tsp. smoked paprika, use hot smoked for more heat
- 1 chicken, baked and shredded
- Salt and pepper to taste
- ¼ cup sweet and hot jalapeño juice, optional
- Blue cheese crumbles and a Cheese Crisp (see page 41), optional

Instructions

1. In a large 6-qt. stockpot, heat the oil and butter on high heat.
2. Add the onion, celery, and carrots. Sauté for 5 minutes.
3. Add the chicken, garlic, salt, pepper, cumin, and paprika. Mix well and let the mixture cook on medium heat for 10 minutes.
4. Add the beer and simmer for 10 minutes.
5. Add the tomatoes, hot sauce, stock, beans, and jalapeño juice. Simmer over low heat for an hour.
6. Serve with the blue cheese crumbles and cheese crisp.

Notes

You can use a rotisserie chicken in place of baking your own. It will be quicker, and you can be assured that it will be flavorful.

I make sure that I use a full-bodied beer rather than a light beer. It adds a deeper flavor to your chili.

Cheese Crisps

These are the perfect accompaniment for soups or salads. They add a rustic look to charcuterie boards and make a great snack! For this recipe, use the cheese you enjoy the most.

Ingredients

- Shredded cheddar or parmesan cheese (hard cheeses will work best)

Instructions

1. Preheat a griddle to 375°F.
2. Place handfuls of the cheese on the griddle, with a little space in between.
3. Let the handfuls melt until the edges are brown, then turn them over. They will be easy to turn once they are brown enough. If you try to turn them too soon, they will stick to the griddle.
4. After you turn them, let the side that is down get brown, then remove them from the heat and drain them on paper towels.
5. For added flavor, sprinkle them while they're still warm with your favorite seasoning.

Notes

If possible, shred or crumble your own cheese. Pre-shredded won't melt as well due to the nonstick agents that are added.

Cheesy Wild Rice and Mushroom Soup

Makes 8 servings

This is one of the most popular soups that we make at the café. It's cheesy, it's creamy, it's full of flavor, and it's very satisfying. You may want to double your batch!

Ingredients

- One 6.6-oz. box wild rice, I use Uncle Ben's Long Grain & Wild Rice
- 1 lb. mushrooms, chopped
- 1 yellow onion, chopped
- ⅓ cup butter
- ⅓ cup flour
- 3 cups half-and-half
- 2 cups chicken stock
- Salt and pepper
- ½–1 tsp. granulated garlic
- 2 cups shredded sharp cheddar
- 1 cup cubed easy-melt cheese, I use Velveeta

Instructions

1. Cook the wild rice according to the package directions, adding the mushrooms prior to cooking. Set aside.
2. In a large pot, over medium heat, melt the butter. Add the onion and cook until soft, about 5 minutes.
3. Whisk in the flour and cook until it is a light golden brown.
4. Lower the heat to medium low and slowly add in and whisk the half-and-half and chicken stock, stirring out any lumps.
5. Season with salt, pepper, and granulated garlic. Cook and stir frequently until the soup thickens. Do not boil.
6. Stir in the cheese until it melts.
7. Add the wild rice and mushroom mixture and stir to incorporate.

Notes

When a recipe calls for shredded cheese, shred your own. Pre-shredded cheese does not melt as well due to the anticaking agents on it. Fresh is always better!

Adding a little easy-melt cheese to your cheese soup creates a creamy texture. Before adding salt, taste-test first. The chicken stock adds salt, as does the wild rice mix.

Mac and Cheese Soup

Makes 5 servings

I threw this soup together one blustery, chilly day at the café with some extra mac and cheese we had on hand. It was such a hit with our guests that we decided to refine the recipe. The base cheese soup recipe makes it easy to experiment with flavors and ingredients. One of the most popular has been mac and cheese with roasted garden peppers. We used banana, poblano, cowhorn, and jalapeño peppers. Have fun with this and don't be afraid to add your favorite ingredients.

Ingredients

- 3 Tbsp. butter
- 1 large onion, diced
- ⅓–½ cup flour
- 1 tsp. granulated garlic
- 7 large russet potatoes, peeled and chopped into 1" cubes
- 2 cups cubed easy-melt cheese, I use Velveeta
- 4 cups chicken broth
- 1½ cups whole milk
- 1½ cups heavy cream
- Salt and pepper, to taste
- 1 tsp. smoked sweet paprika, optional
- Homemade croutons, shredded cheese, green onion, bacon, sour cream, or jalapeños, for garnish

Instructions

1. In a large pot, melt the butter over medium-high heat. Add the onions and cook until they are soft, 4–5 minutes.
2. Sprinkle the flour over the onions and whisk until smooth. Let it cook for 2 minutes on medium heat.
3. Add the remaining ingredients, stir well, and bring to a boil. Reduce the heat to medium and cook until the potatoes break apart with a fork when pierced and the cheese is melted.
4. Reduce the heat to low, take half the soup out and set it aside in a bowl. Use a potato masher to mash the soup remaining in the pot until the potatoes are the desired consistency.
5. Return the set-aside soup to the pot and heat for 10 more minutes prior to serving.
6. Garnish with homemade croutons, shredded cheese, green onion, bacon, sour cream, or jalapeños.

Notes

You can use cheddar, pepper jack, Gouda, smoked, or whatever cheese you like, as long as it melts smooth.

Try adding steamed broccoli, shredded chicken, diced potatoes, or bacon to your soup.

Garnish with shredded cheese, cheese fish crackers, and parsley.

Down-Home Hearty Beef Stew

Makes 8 servings

When I grew up in the Midwest, the winters were cold and the wind chilled you to the bone. It did not seem quite as intolerable when you knew that there was a pot of beef stew simmering on the stove. This classic stew is one that will never go out of style and is guaranteed to warm you up. Grab a loaf of warm crusty bread, and you have a perfect dinner.

Instructions

1. Place the Stew Seasoning Mix in a small bowl and toss the stew meat in it in batches, until all the meat is seasoned. Set the meat aside.

2. In a medium pot, heat 2 Tbsp. of the oil over medium-high heat. Add the meat to the pan in batches, making sure you get a good sear on the meat. Remove the meat and set it aside.

3. Add 1 Tbsp. of the oil to the pan, then add the onion, celery, and garlic. Cook until soft.

4. Add the tomato paste and stir until combined. Add the diced tomatoes, beef broth, Worcestershire sauce, seared beef, and all its juices. Bring this to a boil then turn the heat down and simmer for 2 hours or until the beef is fall-apart tender.

5. Add your potatoes and carrots and simmer until they are tender, about 45 minutes. Stir in the peas and parsley.

6. To thicken your stew, stir together the cornstarch and water, then add it to your stew and cook until the stew thickens.

Notes

You can also add sweet potatoes, green beans, or mushrooms.

If you are a venison fan, use it instead of beef.

The most popular cuts of beef for stew are chuck, short rib, and brisket.

Stew Seasoning Mix

- 1 tsp. kosher salt
- ½ tsp. black pepper
- 1 tsp. paprika
- 1 tsp. thyme
- 1 tsp. marjoram

Ingredients

- 3 Tbsp. vegetable oil, divided
- 3 lbs. beef stew meat
- 1 large yellow onion, chopped
- 4 carrots, peeled and chopped
- 3 celery stalks with leaves, chopped
- 2 cups frozen peas
- 1½ lbs. yellow potatoes, quartered
- 1 tsp. minced garlic
- 4 Tbsp. tomato paste
- One 15-oz. can diced tomatoes
- 4 cups beef broth
- Dash Worcestershire sauce
- 3 Tbsp. fresh parsley, roughly chopped
- ¼ cup water
- 2 Tbsp. cornstarch
- Stew Seasoning Mix, see below

Old-Fashioned Potato Soup

Makes 6 servings

This will not qualify as health food, but it meets all the requirements for delicious comfort food. And that is all that matters!

Instructions

1. In a large pot, melt the butter over medium-high heat. Add the onions and cook until they are soft, 4–5 minutes.

2. Sprinkle the flour over the onions and whisk until smooth. Let it cook for 2 minutes on medium heat.

3. Add the remaining ingredients, stir well, and bring to a boil. Reduce the heat to medium and cook until the potatoes break apart with a fork when pierced and the cheese is melted.

4. Reduce the heat to low, take half the soup out and set it aside in a bowl. Use a potato masher to mash the soup remaining in the pot until the potatoes are the desired consistency.

5. Return the set-aside soup to the pot and heat for 10 more minutes prior to serving.

6. Garnish with homemade croutons, shredded cheese, green onion, bacon, sour cream, or jalapeños.

Notes

When cutting the potatoes, keep them all the same size. This will ensure even cooking.

Anytime you are using a stock base, check the taste of your soup before adding additional salt. These bases normally contain salt already.

You can add bacon or ham to your soup in step 3, if desired.

You want to use a potato that will break down easily like russet or Yukon Gold.

Ingredients

- 3 Tbsp. butter
- 1 large onion, diced
- ⅓–½ cup flour
- 1 tsp. granulated garlic
- 7 large russet potatoes, peeled and chopped into 1" cubes
- 2 cups cubed easy-melt cheese, I use Velveeta
- 4 cups chicken broth
- 1½ cups whole milk
- 1½ cups heavy cream
- Salt and pepper, to taste
- 1 tsp. smoked sweet paprika, optional
- Homemade croutons, shredded cheese, green onion, bacon, sour cream, or jalapeños, for garnish

CHAPTER 5

Hearty Sandwiches

Two slices of bread are the gateway to creative and delicious handheld food, and there is simply no end to what you can put between them. From fresh spreads to leftovers, your next favorite sandwich is just a few favorite ingredients away.

page 57

page 50

page 49

page 56

page 54

Eggcellent Egg Salad

Makes 8–10 servings

The best egg salad begins with fresh eggs. Fresh eggs will make your egg salad look brighter and more beautiful, like a bowl of sunshine. I like egg salad with a little zing, so I use apple cider vinegar in my base. It gives it that little zip. We could call this Zip and Zing Egg Salad!

Ingredients

- 15 eggs, boiled, peeled, and chopped
- 1 cup mayonnaise
- 2 Tbsp. yellow mustard
- ¼ tsp. pepper
- ¼ tsp. celery salt
- ¼ tsp. dill weed
- ½ tsp. chives
- 2 Tbsp. dried parsley
- 1–2 tsp. sugar
- ½ Tbsp. apple cider vinegar
- ¼–½ tsp. Old Bay seasoning
- ¼ tsp. salt

Instructions

1. Whisk together everything but the eggs. Taste and adjust the salt, sugar, and Old Bay as desired.
2. Fold the dressing into the eggs, being careful not to smash them.
3. Refrigerate before serving.

Notes

This can be made into a sandwich, paired with crackers as a snack, or served on toast for breakfast.

If you have extra hard-boiled eggs on hand, this is a great way to use them.

Egg salad is also great piled on a cucumber slice and topped with a sprig of fresh dill.

I like to up the taste game by adding a dash of hot sauce on my egg salad sandwiches.

Café-Style Chicken Salad

Makes 8–10 servings

At our café, selling out of fresh chicken salad is a daily occurrence. It's a crowd-pleaser and we often sell large quantities to our guests for parties or gatherings. It's great to have on hand at home for a quick lunch or snack.

Ingredients

- 2 cups mayonnaise
- 1 tsp. kosher salt
- 1 tsp. black pepper
- 1 tsp. sugar
- ½ Tbsp. dried parsley
- ¼ tsp. granulated garlic
- 8 hard-boiled eggs, peeled and chopped
- 2 stalks celery, diced
- 4–5 cups chicken breasts, baked and shredded (see the Notes on page 38)
- Chopped grapes, apples, or nuts, optional

Instructions

1. In a bowl, mix the mayonnaise, salt, pepper, sugar, parsley, and garlic to make the dressing.
2. Add the eggs, chicken, and celery, and mix well. If the salad is too wet, add more chicken. If it's too dry, add more mayonnaise.
3. Before serving, add diced grapes, apples, or nuts, if desired.

Notes

This salad is great for sandwiches or in lettuce wraps.

If you're short on time, use shredded rotisserie chicken. It will have great flavor already baked in.

For variety, use turkey in place of the chicken.

Mexican BLT

Makes 1 serving

Who doesn't love a great BLT? The crispy bacon, red ripe tomatoes, and creamy mayonnaise's texture and flavor contrast is a gift for your mouth. But what if we switched it up a bit? Well, I was at one of my favorite Mexican restaurants and had a dish with jicama strips on it, and wow! I decided that I was going to take my BLT in a new direction with some added texture and cool sweet flavor.

Notes

Jicama has juicy and crunchy flesh and it's a little sweet and slightly nutty. The texture is kind of like a pear.

Until 2019, the BLT was ranked as the second most popular sandwich in the US. In 2019, it dropped to number six (the grilled cheese takes top honors).

You can panfry your bacon or cook it in the oven, which I think is easier and creates less mess.

Ingredients

- 2 slices sourdough bread
- 3–4 thick tomato slices
- 2–3 lettuce leaves
- Cilantro sprigs
- 5–6 slices bacon, seasoned with chili pepper blend, I use Olde Virden's Red Hot Sprinkle
- 1 jicama
- 3 Tbsp. mayonnaise
- 1 tsp. lime juice
- Salt and pepper
- ½ tsp. avocado oil
- ⅛ tsp. garlic powder

Instructions

1. Toast your bread, if desired, then set it aside.
2. Make the Mexican mayonnaise by putting the mayonnaise, lime juice, salt and pepper, avocado oil, and garlic powder in a small bowl. Whisk until well blended. Taste and adjust the seasoning as desired.
3. Cook your bacon until it reaches your desired crispiness, then drain the fat, sprinkle it with the chili pepper blend, and set it aside.
4. Cut your jicama into long thin slices.
5. Assemble your sandwich by spreading a layer of mayonnaise on each slice of bread, then layer on one side the bacon, lettuce, cilantro, tomato, and jicama.
6. Add the other slice of bread on tip, cut in half, and enjoy!

Meatloaf Sliders

Makes 3–4 servings

Sliders are an essential part of American cuisine, whether they are beef, chicken, ham, or turkey. I started making sliders when my kids were little because they were easy for their small hands to hold. I realized that those small buns opened the door for creativity with leftovers and your favorite sandwich fixins!

Ingredients

- One 8-pack slider buns, I use yeast or sweet Hawaiian varieties
- Leftover meatloaf (see Meatloaf and Mashed Potato Bowl recipe on page 79)
- Red onion, raw or pickled (see Pickled Red Onions recipe on page 53)
- Barbecue sauce
- Thin sharp cheddar cheese slices
- Melted butter

Instructions

1. Cut the buns in half and place the bottom halves in a pan, set aside.
2. Preheat the oven to 350°F.
3. Cut your meatloaf into bun-size pieces and place a generous portion on the bottom half of each bun.
4. Top each meatloaf slice with a slice of cheese, barbecue sauce, and red onion.
5. Place the top of the bun on the assembled slider.
6. Using a pastry brush, cover the top of each bun with butter.
7. Cover with foil and bake for 20 minutes or until the cheese melts.

Notes

Sliders originated in the 1940s when Navy sailors referred to their small burgers as sliders because of their extreme greasiness!

A slider is traditionally a small burger, around 2" in diameter.

In the late 1870s, the first meatloaf recipe was recorded. Because it used bread and eggs, however, it was presented as a breakfast option.

Pickled Red Onions

Makes 4 cups

Pickled red onions are easy to make, so versatile, and add such a flavor pop to anything you add them to. I like to keep a jar or two in my refrigerator all the time.

Instructions

1. Before you start slicing the onions, boil 6 cups of water and keep on the stove top.
2. Peel and slice your onions into thin ¼" sections.
3. In the jars that you will use to store your pickled onions, divide and add the sugar, salt, and vinegar, stirring well to dissolve.
4. Put your onions in a colander in the sink and pour the boiling water over them, letting them drain. This will par-blanch the onions.
5. Place the onions in the jars and stir well.
6. They can be eaten in about an hour but are better if left to sit overnight.

Ingredients

- 2 medium red onions
- 1 tsp. sugar
- 1 tsp. salt
- 1½–2 cups vinegar, I use rice vinegar, white wine vinegar, or apple cider vinegar
- 2 medium jars with lids, for storage

Notes

Add seasonings or spices to the jar. I suggest trying garlic cloves, whole peppercorns, or dried peppers.

These are great on any sandwich, in tacos, on charcuterie boards, as a garnish, or in salads.

Ultimate Comfort Grilled Cheese
Makes 1–4 serving

I happen to adore cheese, so when I prepare a grilled cheese, I want cheese on top of cheese on top of cheese. For me, it's the combination of the crispy exterior of the perfectly toasted bread and the creamy interior of the melted cheese. What else could bring comfort like this?

Ingredients
- 2 slices of sourdough bread, sliced to ⅝" thick
- 6 slices of a good melty cheese (see Notes below)
- Melted butter

Instructions
1. Heat the griddle to 350°F.
2. Using a pastry brush, butter one side of each slice of bread and place them buttered side down on the griddle.
3. Put three slices of cheese on each slice of bread.
4. Wait patiently until the cheese has melted and the bread is golden brown. Use a spatula to put the halves of the sandwich together.
5. Remove the sandwich from the griddle, cut it in half, and enjoy dipping into some Tomato Basil Soup (see page 55).

Notes
Great melting cheese options include American, provolone, pepper jack, mild cheddar, Gouda, or Havarti.

Make sure your griddle is hot so that your sandwich doesn't become soggy.

Tomato Basil Soup

Makes 10 servings

This is the all-American soup. We loved it as kids, and we crave it as adults. Whether you are dunking your grilled cheese in it or floating cheese fish crackers on top, this soup is warm and comforting and feels like coming home.

Instructions

1. Pour the tomato soup into a large pot over medium-high heat. Add the hot water.
2. Add the crushed tomatoes and tomato paste and stir well. Add the salt, cayenne pepper, black pepper, and garlic. Stir well to incorporate.
3. Add the pesto to the soup and stir well.
4. Add the remaining whole milk, stirring to mix. Do not let the soup come to a boil.

Notes

Experiment by using fresh basil instead of pesto.

There are several varieties of basil that you can use like sweet basil, Thai basil, or Genovese basil.

Ingredients

- One 75-oz. package condensed tomato soup
- 4½ cups hot water
- One 14-oz. can crushed tomatoes
- One 6-oz. can tomato paste
- ½ tsp. salt
- ⅛ tsp. cayenne pepper
- ¼ tsp. black pepper
- ½ Tbsp. granulated garlic
- 1½ cups whole milk
- 2 Tbsp. pesto

Pumpkin Butter Grilled Cheese

Makes 2 servings

I look forward to fall every year. I do not know whether it is the beauty of the turning leaves on the hillside, the local farmers proudly displaying their pumpkins, or the sheer joy I find in Fall comfort cooking. Pumpkin butter is one of the first things I cook for the café every fall to accompany our proudly featured Pumpkin Butter Grilled Cheese.

Ingredients

- 4 slices hearty sourdough bread
- Melted butter
- 8 slices provolone or Swiss cheese
- 8 slices of deli-style ham, turkey, or precooked crispy bacon
- Pumpkin butter
- Cinnamon sugar, optional

Instructions

1. Preheat your griddle to 350°F.
2. Butter one side of each slice of bread and place them butter side down on the griddle.
3. Put two slices of cheese on each slice of bread.
4. On two slices of the bread, spread about 2 Tbsp. of your pumpkin butter, making sure to spread it to the edges.
5. On top of the pumpkin butter, add your protein of choice.
6. When the cheese is melted and the bread is golden brown, use your spatula to put the bread together.
7. Remove the sandwiches from the griddle, cut them, and enjoy a taste of fall!
8. If you desire, top the sandwich with a dusting of cinnamon sugar.

Notes

You can make this sandwich with any protein you want, or simply enjoy it with cheese and pumpkin butter.

Experiment with various bread options, such as rye or pumpernickel.

Mac and Cheese Toasted Wrap

Makes 2 servings

This wrap encompasses everything that I love about the experience of eating. It excites the senses with its creamy, crunchy, salty, and spicy elements. Excuse me while I drool.

Instructions

1. Heat a griddle or large skillet to 350°F.
2. Lay your 12" tortilla flat and add about ½ cup of cheese to the center.
3. On top of that cheese, place one of the tostado shells.
4. Put about ½–¾ cup of macaroni and cheese on the tostado shell. This is where you can add additional ingredients. Be careful to not overfill it otherwise it will not close.
5. Place the other corn tostada shell on top of the mac and cheese.
6. Top the tostada off with about ¼–½ cup of shredded cheese.
7. Working around the edges, close the tortilla over itself. It's ok if it overlaps.
8. Put butter in your pan or on your griddle and place the wrap folded side down. Put something heavy on top of it and let it cook undisturbed for about 3–4 minutes.
9. Butter the top of your wrap, then turn it over and repeat the process.
10. When your wrap is toasty brown and crispy on both sides, remove it from the heat and enjoy!

Ingredients

- 4 corn tostado shells
- Two 12" flour tortillas
- Mac and Cheese (see the recipes on pages 94–96)
- 3 cups shredded cheese
- Melted butter
- Ranch dressing, for dipping

Notes

You can add so many tasty things to your wrap prior to grilling it. I suggest trying onions, jalapeños, peppers, cilantro, avocado, chicken, or beef. It's fun to make several varieties.

Your dipping sauce can be anything that you enjoy. Try using queso, salsa, or a jalapeño ranch!

Use any macaroni and cheese variety that you like from just plain cheese or buffalo mac to blue cheese or Mexican mac and cheese.

CHAPTER 6

Childhood Comforts

There are certain dishes and familiar aromas that transport us back to childhood gatherings around the table, with grandma in her apron, serving the whole family. In collecting these memories to share with you I was flooded with nostalgic moments that made me smile.

page 66

page 65

page 67

page 72

Homemade Lasagna

Makes 10 servings

I started making this lasagna for my family when I was in the sixth grade. I have refined it and recently added the pepperoni. I like the texture and the little bit of spice and extra flavor that it adds. This sauce is best if you make it one day and let it sit and use it the next. That gives all those wonderful flavors and spices time to hang out and get to know each other. Funny story, my mom once asked me to make this for company that we were expecting, but being the busy teen that I was, I didn't "have time." I reluctantly got in the kitchen and was in such a hurry that I added 3 cups of sugar instead of 3 teaspoons. It was still delicious, but a little on the sweet side.

Instructions

1. In a large Dutch oven or stock pot cook the ground beef and onions until the beef is brown and there is no pink. Drain the fat.
2. Add the tomatoes, tomato paste, water, garlic, salt, oregano, basil, rosemary, and sugar. Bring to a boil then simmer, all day if you can.
3. When ready to assemble, preheat the oven to 350°F. Grease a 9" x 13" pan.
4. Boil the noodles as directed on the package, drain them, and set them aside.
5. Put a piece of parchment on a cookie sheet and lay the pepperoni on the pan. Bake until they are brown on the edges. Drain on paper towels and set aside.
6. Spread a layer of your prepared sauce on the bottom of the pan.
7. Add a layer of noodles on top.
8. Add a layer of the ricotta or cottage cheese and mozzarella.
9. Spread a layer of the sauce and all the pepperoni.
10. Repeat the layering with the final layer being noodles, meat sauce, mozzarella, and parmesan cheese.
11. Bake at 350°F until the cheese is melted, bubbly, and brown around the edges.
12. Let sit for about 15 minutes before cutting and serving.

Notes

You can use all ground beef or a mixture of beef and sausage.

One theory says that "lasagna" was derived from the ancient Greek word *laganon*, which was an early pastry, perhaps the first form of pasta. It was possibly flat sheets cut into thin strips.

Make sure you have leftovers, as next-day lasagna is *deliziosa!*

Ingredients

- 2 lbs. ground beef
- 1 small package medium or large sliced pepperoni pieces
- 1½ cups diced white or yellow onions
- One 28-oz. can diced tomatoes
- One 12-oz. can tomato paste
- 2 cups water
- 1–2 large garlic cloves, crushed
- 1 Tbsp. salt
- 1½ tsp. oregano leaves
- 1½ tsp. basil leaves
- ½ tsp. rosemary leaves
- 3 tsp. sugar
- One 1-lb. box lasagna noodles
- 3 cups ricotta or cottage cheese
- 1½ cups parmesan cheese
- 4 cups shredded mozzarella cheese

Chili Beans and Rice

Makes 8 servings

My brother and sister and I always looked forward to this dish. It's so amazingly simple, but to me, it tasted like a million bucks. This recipe reminds me of my mom and the love that she put into everything she made for us. This meal is not complete for me without soft white bread covered in tasty butter. Honestly y'all, I can taste it right now.

Ingredients

- 1 lb. enriched white rice or long-grain wild rice
- 1 lb. ground beef
- Two 15-oz. cans of chili beans, undrained
- 1 medium white onion, chopped, optional
- ½–1 cup ketchup
- Salt and pepper to taste
- Chopped parsley, for garnish

Instructions

1. Cook the rice according to the package directions, and set it aside.
2. In a large skillet, brown the ground beef and onions. When brown, drain the fat.
3. Add the rice and chili beans to the skillet. Stir well.
4. Add the ketchup, mix well, and serve warm.

Notes

The ketchup adds kick to this dish without having to add additional spices; plus I love ketchup!

Did you know that adding 1 cup of beans to your recipe adds about 15g of protein?

For a delicious variation, top with shredded cheese or a fried egg.

If you do not like chili beans, you can substitute black beans or pinto beans.

Ruth's Cheeseburger Pies—Taco-Style

Chef Chris Grove, Certified Food Judge for the World Food Championships and BBQ Cookbook Author

Makes 12 cheeseburger pies

I would come running to the dinner table when I was a kid and my mom would make cheeseburger pies. They were deliciously cheesy and crusty handheld pies filled with ground beef, onions, and cheese. This is my taco-style variation of these gooey pockets of goodness.

Ingredients

- 1 Tbsp. oil
- ½ cup diced onion
- ½ cup diced red bell pepper
- 2 cloves garlic, peeled and minced
- 1 lb. fresh ground chuck
- 1 Tbsp. fajita seasoning
- 6 oz. Oaxaca cheese (you can substitute mozzarella)
- One 8-ct. package biscuits, I use Grands!
- 1 egg white
- 1 Tbsp. cold water

Instructions

1. Preheat a skillet over medium-high heat. Add the oil and sauté the onion and bell pepper for 2–3 minutes. Add the garlic and ground beef. Cook, breaking up with a spoon, until the beef is browned. Remove from heat and drain the fat.

2. On a floured surface, roll out a biscuit into a 5" circle. Lightly dampen the edges of the circle. Top with 2–3 Tbsp. of the meat mixture and 1–2 Tbsp. of shredded cheese. Fold one edge of the biscuit over the filling to the opposite edge, forming a closed semicircle. Press the tines of a fork down on the edges to crimp them closed. Use the fork or a sharp knife to poke 3 holes on the top of the pie. Repeat with the remaining biscuits.

3. Preheat a grill set up for indirect heat or an oven set to 425°F. Make an egg wash by mixing the egg white and water together, then brush it onto the pies. Place the pies on a pan and place the pan in the grill or oven. Cook until the crust is golden brown, about 8–12 minutes.

Scalloped Potatoes and Ham

Makes 12 servings

Are you craving something tender, creamy, and comforting? Grab that sack of potatoes and slice that leftover ham because these scalloped potatoes and ham are full of flavor and are certain to make you smile on the inside and out.

Instructions

1. Preheat the oven to 325°F and spray a large casserole dish with cooking spray.

2. In a large skillet, melt the butter over medium heat, then whisk in the flour, salt, and pepper until smooth. Add the half-and-half slowly and stir until the mixture starts to thicken.

3. Add half of the mozzarella cheese and stir until melted.

4. Put a thin layer of sauce in the bottom of your casserole dish. Arrange ⅓ of the sliced potatoes on top, then add more sauce, onions, cheddar cheese, and ham. Repeat this process until your casserole dish is full.

5. Top with the last of the cheddar and mozzarella cheeses.

6. Cover with foil and bake for 45 minutes, then uncover and bake for 20 minutes more or until the potatoes are tender and the cheese starts to brown.

7. Sprinkle with parsley or chives before serving.

Ingredients

- 4 Tbsp. all-purpose flour
- 4 Tbsp. butter
- 2 tsp. salt
- Black pepper to taste
- 4 cups half-and-half
- 3 cups shredded cheddar cheese, I use sharp cheddar
- 2 cups shredded mozzarella
- 2 small yellow onions, thinly sliced
- 4 lbs. russet potatoes sliced ⅛" thick (if you do not peel them, scrub them well)
- 1½–2 lbs. cooked ham, sliced or cubed
- Parsley or chives for garnish, optional

Notes

Try to keep your potato sliced thin so that they cook evenly.

To peel or not to peel? That is a personal choice. If you are not peeling your potatoes, make sure you scrub them well under cold water and remove any blemishes or sprouts.

Take your scalloped potatoes and ham to the next level by playing with various cheese flavors.

Southern Black-Eyed Peas and Ham

Makes 12–15 servings

I can still smell the pot of black-eyed peas cooking all day on my grandmother's stove. I was barely tall enough to see over the huge stock pot that she cooked them in. She would ladle a helping for me, and I would sit at the table in the kitchen, which had a strawberry tablecloth to match the strawberry curtains. I'd happily eat while she busied herself tidying up. She made them with garden-fresh peas that I helped snap, and that made the difference. This is my adapted recipe, but hers were the absolute best.

Instructions

1. Prep your beans by rinsing them and sorting out the bad ones. You can speed up the cooking process by soaking them in water overnight or preboiling them for 3 minutes, covering them, and setting them aside for an hour. Either way, drain the peas before using.

2. In your soup pot, add the oil over medium-high heat and sauté the onions and carrots until tender.

3. Add the bacon, garlic, cayenne, and pepper, cook for 1–2 minutes.

4. Add the broth, ham, and peas and bring to a boil. Reduce the heat and simmer for about 1 hour or until the peas are tender.

5. If you are using ham hocks, remove them from the pot and let them cool slightly. Remove the ham from the bones and return the ham to the pot.

6. Garnish with fresh chopped parsley and serve with warm Country Cornbread (see page 28) and Honey Butter (see page 25).

Ingredients

- 1 lb. dry black-eyed peas
- 1 large yellow or white onion, chopped
- 1 cup diced carrot
- 6 slices smoked bacon, cut into small pieces
- 1 Tbsp. oil
- 3 garlic cloves, minced
- ½ tsp. cayenne pepper
- 32 oz. chicken broth
- 16 oz. beef broth
- Salt and pepper, to taste
- 2 ham hocks or 4 cups cooked and chopped ham

Notes

Some of these ingredients have a solid salt content already. Do not salt your beans until they are done and you've tasted them, otherwise you may end up with oversalted beans and ham.

There is a long-standing tradition of eating black-eyed peas on New Year's Day. It is believed to bring good luck for the new year. For the best chance of good luck, one must eat exactly 365 peas!

Taco Pizza

Makes 8 servings

I grew up in the Midwest, and we indulged ourselves with Happy Joe's Pizza & Ice Cream as often as we could. They have the absolute best taco pizza and bubblegum ice cream. Moving to Tennessee, 15 hours away, had us longing for and reminiscing about the taste of that pizza. I took my family's broken pizza hearts into my own hands and created this taco pizza that is just about, but not quite, as good as Happy Joe's.

Instructions

1. Heat your oven to 450°F. Grease your sheet pan, sprinkle it with cornmeal, and stretch the dough to fit the pan. Bake it for 15 minutes, then remove it from the oven.

2. In a skillet, brown the ground beef and drain the fat. Add the taco seasoning and cook as directed.

3. In a small bowl, mix the refried beans and pizza sauce until they are well mixed. Spread the mixture evenly over the pizza crust.

4. Add the taco meat on top of the sauce.

5. Top the meat with 3 cups of cheddar cheese and bake until the cheese melts and the crust is brown and crispy on the edges. Remove it from the oven.

6. Top with lettuce, shredded cheddar cheese, and Doritos. Slice it into squares and serve with additional taco toppings, as desired. It's perfect served with a side of guacamole and chips!

Ingredients

- Pizza dough to fill an 11" x 15" sheet pan
- 1 lb. ground beef
- 1 packet of taco seasoning mix
- One 15-oz. can refried beans
- 2 cups pizza sauce
- 1 head of iceberg lettuce, chopped
- 6 cups shredded cheddar cheese
- 2 tomatoes, chopped
- 1 large yellow onion, diced
- Sour cream
- Jalapeños, pickled or fresh
- Black olives, sliced
- Taco sauce
- 1 large bag cheese tortilla chips, crushed, I use Nacho Cheese Doritos

Notes

Local grocery stores now carry pizza dough in the deli section. If you can't find any there, hit up your favorite pizza joint for a ball of fresh dough.

Iowa Loose Meat Sandwiches
Makes 10 servings

I spent some of my years in Ottumwa, Iowa, and food from The Canteen restaurant was a weekly must-have for lunch. Many of us who have moved away and go back to visit make this our first stop. If you have been there, you know why. This is my version of their perfected sandwich. They've been in business for 95 years!

Ingredients
- 3 lbs. ground beef
- 2 small white onions, diced
- 2 beef bouillon cubes
- 1 chicken bouillon cube
- 1½ cups water
- 2½ Tbsp. brown sugar
- 2 Tbsp. apple cider vinegar
- 2½ Tbsp. Worcestershire sauce
- 1 Tbsp. soy sauce
- 1 tsp. black pepper

Instructions
1. Add all the ingredients to a slow cooker.
2. Mix well to incorporate all the ingredients and to break up the meat.
3. Simmer on low heat all day, until the meat is no longer pink.
4. The goal is to steam the meat, not fry it.
5. Serve on a fresh hamburger bun with your favorite condiments.

Notes
The condiments you can use are as varied as the people who love loose meat sandwiches—it's been known to cause whole debates! I am a fan of mustard, pickles, and onions.

The goal is to steam, not fry, the meat. When done it will be sitting in juices, and that is ok. Use a slotted spoon to place the meat on the bun.

If you are serving a group, put several sandwiches together and then back into the bag that the buns were in and seal it for 2–3 minutes. The heat from the meat will steam the buns!

Open-Faced Hot Roast Beef Sandwich

Makes 4 servings

My mom made roasts for us frequently, usually for Sunday lunch after church. Not only was it mouthwatering then, but the meals with leftovers were something to look forward to. This open-faced sandwich was one. If I was really lucky, there would be a cold roast beef and ketchup sandwich on squishy white bread in my lunchbox. Best lunch ever!

Ingredients

- 3 cups beef broth or leftover broth from cooking your roast
- 6 Tbsp. flour
- 3 Tbsp. butter
- 8 slices soft white sandwich bread
- Mashed Potatoes (see page 69)
- Leftover pot roast (see Sunday Pot Roast recipe on page 84)
- Green onions for garnish

Instructions

1. Add the butter and flour to a saucepan over medium-high heat and whisk until it forms what looks like a paste. This will take about 2 minutes.
2. Slowly add 2 cups of beef liquid while whisking, to prevent lumps. When smooth, add the remaining beef liquid. If you are using beef broth, add seasonings (see Notes below).
3. Let the gravy cook until it thickens.
4. Lay two slices of bread on a plate and add a heaping serving of mashed potatoes. Lay the roast beef on top of the potatoes and top it all off with a river of gravy. Garnish with green onions.

Notes

When you make a roast, save the pan drippings for gravy.

If you are using beef broth, you may have to season your gravy more than if you are using pan drippings. Add ½ tsp. of garlic powder and ½ tsp. onion powder. Then finish with salt and pepper to taste.

Mashed Potatoes

Makes 10 servings

Mashed potatoes are the top requested side from everyone at any family gathering that we have. I like to occasionally switch up the flavor profile by adding more seasoning, shredded cheese, or crispy bacon.

Ingredients

- 5 lbs. Yukon Gold potatoes
- 1 cup sour cream
- 1 stick butter, room temperature
- Salt and pepper
- 4–5 cloves garlic, minced
- 1 cup half-and-half
- Fresh chopped chives

Instructions

1. Wash and rinse the potatoes, cut them into 1" cubes, and place them in a pot of cold water as you cut them.

2. Add 1 Tbsp. of salt and bring the pot to a boil. Once it is boiling, lower the heat to medium and cook until the potatoes are soft.

3. Drain the water off the potatoes and add butter, sour cream, garlic, and salt and pepper. Mash them with either a potato masher or a handheld electric mixer. Do not overmix—you want to leave a few chunks in the potatoes.

4. Look at the texture of your potatoes and if they are thicker than you would like, add half-and-half and mash again.

5. When they are the perfect texture for you, stir in fresh chopped chives and serve.

Cindy's Tater Tot Casserole

Makes 8 servings

Having fussy eaters is something that most parents deal with. This casserole that my stepmom made for us, more for the kids, was guaranteed to please even the pickiest of eaters. The tasty, crunchy tots distracted them from the vegetables buried below.

Instructions

1. Preheat the oven to 350°F.
2. In a skillet, brown the ground beef and onion, drain the fat, and season with salt and pepper.
3. Put the mixture in a large bowl.
4. Defrost the frozen vegetables enough to thaw but not cook them.
5. Add the vegetables, soup, and cheese to the hamburger mixture and mix well.
6. Defrost the tater tots for about 4 minutes. Put them in a bowl and toss them with the ranch seasoning.
7. Place the hamburger mix in a 9" x 13" pan, then place the seasoned tater tots on top.
8. Cover with foil and bake for 1 hour. Remove the foil and bake for 30 minutes more or until the tots are brown and crispy.

Notes

Seasoning the tater tots is optional, and you can use a variety of seasoning mixes like onion and garlic, parmesan cheese, or a general seasoned salt.

Add a dash of hot sauce to your portion for an extra kick.

Americans consume approximately 70 million pounds of tater tots per year.

Ingredients

- 2 lbs. ground beef
- 1 large yellow onion, diced
- 24 oz. frozen mixed vegetables (corn, peas, green beans, and carrots)
- 32 oz. frozen tater tots
- Two 10½-oz. cans cream of mushroom or cream of chicken soup
- ½ lb. easy-melt cheese, cubed, I use Velveeta
- Salt and pepper
- 2–3 Tbsp. ranch seasoning

Grandma's Chocolate Cream Pie

Makes 6–8 servings

My grandmother, my most favorite person in the world, lived in Texas and we lived in Iowa. Every summer we would visit her and upon our arrival she always had three things ready for me: a big pot of black-eyed peas (fresh from her garden), a pitcher of Tang in the door of the refrigerator, and a chocolate pie. These memories of her make my heart so happy. Love you, Grandma.

Instructions

1. Mix the cocoa, flour, milk, and egg yolks. Cook over medium heat, stirring regularly, until the mixture is thick.

2. Add the butter and vanilla and stir well. Set aside to cool.

3. When the mixture is cool, stir in the chocolate chips.

4. Put the mixture in the prebaked pie shell and garnish with whipped cream, if desired.

Notes

You can also use the pie filling to make pudding parfaits.

Make a chocolate banana pie by adding sliced bananas to the baked pie shell prior to adding in the chocolate filling.

You can make your own whipped cream (see the recipe for a coffee-flavored version on page 112).

Ingredients

- 1½ cups sugar
- 5 Tbsp. flour
- 2 egg yolks, beaten
- ½ stick butter
- 5 Tbsp. cocoa powder
- 2 cups whole milk
- 1 Tbsp. vanilla extract
- 1 cup mini chocolate chips
- Prebaked 9" pie shell
- Whipped cream for topping, optional

Texas Apricot Balls

Makes 12–15 servings

My grandmother had an apricot tree in her backyard, and besides spoiling me with the best jam, she would make apricot balls. When I would visit, there were neighbor kids that I would spend time with, and she always made them for us. To this day, Sandra (one of these neighbor kids) remembers my grandmother making those apricot balls for us.

Ingredients

- One 12-oz. package dried apricots, finely chopped
- Juice of one medium orange
- 2 cups toasted sweetened coconut
- 2 cups powdered sugar

Instructions

1. Mix all the ingredients, except for the powdered sugar, together in a bowl and roll them into walnut-sized balls.

2. Roll the balls in the powdered sugar and place them on a parchment-covered baking sheet.

3. You can eat them right away or store them in an airtight container in the refrigerator for one week.

Notes

To toast your coconut, preheat your oven to 325°F and spread the coconut in a thin layer on a baking sheet and bake. Watch carefully as it will only take 5–8 minutes. Toast until lightly browned. Cool completely.

To get the most juice from your orange, heat it in the microwave for 10 seconds, then roll it with the palm of your hand across the counter, cut it, and squeeze!

California produces about 95% of the apricots in the United States.

CHAPTER 7

Memorable Main Dishes

A main dish, to me, means a meal that someone put a lot of thought and love into cooking—something you can sit and enjoy together. Family meals encourage conversation and a sense of belonging while relieving stress. Isn't that what comfort food is all about?

page 92

page 76

page 80

page 77

page 90

Chicken and Spinach Pasta Bake

Makes 8 servings

I am not much of a white-sauce pasta fan, but this pasta bake is the exception. Because this white sauce is so cheesy and seasoned perfectly with Italian herbs, it is easy to love. This is a versatile sauce, as well—you can make a pasta bake, lasagna, or even spaghetti with it. Keep your warm crusty bread on standby— you will want it to sop up the extra sauce.

Ingredients

- 1 lb. penne pasta
- ½ cup butter
- 1 medium white onion, chopped
- 2 cloves garlic, minced
- ½ cup flour
- 1 tsp. salt
- 2 cups chicken broth
- 1½ cups whole milk
- 4 cups mozzarella or Monterey Jack shredded cheese, divided
- 1 cup parmesan cheese
- 1 tsp. basil
- 1 tsp. oregano
- ½ tsp. black pepper
- 2 cups shredded chicken
- 1½ cups ricotta cheese, optional
- 20 oz. chopped, cooked spinach, drained
- Chopped parsley, for garnish

Notes

Make this dish vegetarian by omitting the chicken and using vegetable stock.

Substitute the white sauce for red sauce, if desired.

To kick up the flavor profile a bit, you can add crushed red pepper flakes to your sauce.

Instructions

1. Preheat the oven to 350°F. Boil a pot of water, lightly salted, and add the penne pasta. Cook until al dente. You don't want to overcook the noodles. Drain and rinse them.

2. In a large saucepan, over medium-high heat, melt the butter. Add the onion and cook them until tender. Add the garlic and cook for 1 more minute.

3. Add the flour and salt, stirring until they get thick. Slowly add the milk and broth, stirring constantly with a whisk. Heat to boiling, then turn the heat to medium.

4. Stir in 2 cups of shredded cheese and ½ cup of parmesan cheese. Stir well until the cheese melts.

5. Add the basil, oregano, and pepper. Take the saucepan off the heat and set it aside.

6. In a well-greased casserole dish, add ⅓ of the sauce in the bottom, then add ⅓ of the noodles, the chicken, and ricotta, if using.

7. Add another ⅓ of the sauce over the chicken and add the spinach and 1 cup of mozzarella.

8. Add the rest of the noodles and sauce, then sprinkle with the remaining shredded cheese and parmesan.

9. Bake for 35 minutes or until the cheese is bubbly. Garnish with the chopped parsley.

Spaghetti

Makes 12 servings

Ingredients

- 2 Tbsp. olive oil
- 6 cups chopped sweet onions
- 1 Tbsp. sugar
- 1 lb. ground beef, optional
- ½ cup red wine, optional
- 2 tsp. dried oregano
- 1 tsp. salt
- ½ tsp. thyme
- ½ tsp. marjoram
- ½–1 tsp. basil
- ½ tsp. black pepper
- ¼ tsp. crushed red pepper flakes
- 6 cloves crushed garlic
- Two 28-oz. cans crushed tomatoes
- Two 14½-oz. cans diced tomatoes
- 12 oz. tomato paste
- Shaved or grated parmesan cheese
- Fresh basil

Notes

You can use fresh herbs instead of dried herbs, but you will need to use more as dried herbs have a more concentrated flavor.

You can also use granulated garlic instead of crushed cloves. Use ¼ tsp. for each clove. Fresh garlic cloves have a sweeter and more subtle flavor.

If you prefer, substitute tomato juice for the red wine.

Add any meatballs to your spaghetti after you put it in your serving dish.

Spaghetti ranks as one of my top five favorite foods. This is a recipe that needs to be slow-cooked for as long as possible so that all these beautiful ingredients and flavors have time to play off of one another.

Instructions

1. In a large stockpot, heat 1 Tbsp. olive oil on medium-high heat. Add the onion and sugar. Cook for 30 minutes. If you are using ground beef, add it and cook it until brown. Using a large spoon, remove the fat from the mixture.
2. Add the wine, if using, and cook for 5 minutes.
3. Add the remaining ingredients, bring to a boil, then simmer for at least 3 hours.
4. Boil and prepare the pasta according to the package directions.
5. Place your pasta in a serving dish, cover it with your sauce, and garnish with the fresh basil and shaved parmesan.

Blue Cheese Grits
with Buffalo Chicken

Makes 6 servings

Grits are an extremely versatile food and a Southern comfort staple. Lovers of grits often season them with cheese, butter, and salt. It is said that 96% of Americans are crazy about cheese but 34% just do not like blue cheese, and I agree that it is an acquired taste. So, for all my blue cheese fans out there, enjoy!

Instructions

1. Bake your favorite brand of chicken tenders as directed.
2. In a medium bowl, whisk together the hot sauce, melted butter, and Old Bay.
3. Place the tenders in the sauce two at a time and toss them to coat. Continue until all the tenders are coated.
4. In a large pot over medium heat, add the chicken stock until warm.
5. Add the grits, salt, and pepper and whisk to incorporate.
6. Turn the heat to low and simmer for 20 minutes, or as directed on the grits package. If needed, add more stock to achieve the desired consistency.
7. Remove the pot from the heat and stir in 5 oz. of the blue cheese. Stir until melted and set aside.
8. Using a large spoon, add grits to a serving bowl or plate and sprinkle with celery and carrots if desired. Top with the chicken tenders and sprinkle with the remaining blue cheese.
9. Garnish with parsley or chives.

Notes

Substitute shrimp for the chicken, if desired.

If you are concerned about the blue cheese discoloring white grits, you can use yellow.

Don't like blue cheese? Try using cheddar or a smoked cheese.

Ingredients

- 4 cups chicken stock
- 1 cup slow-cooking corn grits
- ½ tsp. salt
- ½ tsp. pepper
- 6 oz. blue cheese, crumbled and divided
- Celery, finely diced, optional
- Carrots, shredded, optional
- 12 chicken tenders, cooked
- 2 cups Buffalo hot sauce, I use Frank's RedHot
- ½ cup melted butter
- 1 tsp. Old Bay seasoning
- Parsley or chives, chopped, for garnish

Meatloaf and Mashed Potato Bowl

Makes 8 servings

Meatloaf is one of the most comforting and homey meals for my family. The consensus here is that it should be served over chunky mashed potatoes with corn mixed in and the best bite is one that incorporates all three elements! You can enjoy meatloaf sandwiches the next day, too—that is if you are fortunate enough to have any leftovers.

Instructions

1. Preheat the oven to 350°F.
2. In a small bowl, combine the ketchup, brown sugar, and mustard. Mix well and set aside. This will be used to top the meatloaf.
3. In a small pan, add the oil and sauté the onions until they are soft.
4. In a large bowl, mix the onions, crackers, cheese, eggs, milk, salt, and pepper.
5. Add the beef and mix until combined. This is easiest done by hand, to ensure you don't overmix.
6. Place your mixture into a loaf pan and bake for 30 minutes.
7. Remove the pan from the oven and brush on half of the topping. Bake for another 30–40 minutes, until the meat reaches 155°F.
8. Remove from the oven and brush on the remaining topping. Let it rest for 15 minutes, it should reach 160°F–165°F.
9. Place a serving of mashed potatoes topped with a serving of corn in your serving plates or bowls. Add a generous slice of meatloaf.

Ingredients

- ¾ cup ketchup
- 2 Tbsp. light brown sugar
- 1½ tsp. yellow mustard
- 1 Tbsp. olive or vegetable oil
- ¾ cup yellow onion, diced
- 2 lbs. 80% lean ground beef
- 45 butter crackers, crushed
- 3 oz. sharp cheddar cheese, shredded
- 2 oz. pepper jack cheese, shredded
- 3 eggs, whisked
- ½ cup whole milk
- 1 tsp. salt
- ¼ tsp black pepper
- Mashed Potatoes (see recipe on page 69)
- Corn, fresh or frozen

Notes

When making meatloaf, take care to not overwork the meat. Doing so will cause it to be tough.

Always let the meatloaf rest for at least 15 minutes before you cut it. This will seal in the juices.

Bake your meatloaf on a rack, or in a loaf pan with an insert in it so that the fat can drain. You can also put slices of bread under the meatloaf prior to baking to soak up the excess oil.

Ritz crackers work well in this recipe. For added flavor, try using Ritz Garlic Butter Crackers.

For variety, use a combination of ground beef and sausage.

Roasted Veggie Pie

Makes 2 pies

This is a flavorful variation on the Tomato Pie. Use your fresh spring and summer vegetables and be proud to serve this beautiful pie.

Instructions

1. Slice the tomatoes thin and lay them in a large colander. Salt them well and let them drain into the sink for an hour. After they've drained, place them on paper towels and pat them dry.
2. Mix the mayonnaise, vinegar, garlic, cheeses, salt, and pepper.
3. Put a layer of tomatoes and roasted vegetables in the pie shell.
4. Top the vegetables with part of the mayonnaise and cheese mixture.
5. Add another layer of tomatoes and roasted vegetables and finish with the mayonnaise and cheese mixture.
6. Lay pieces of roasted vegetables on top and sprinkle with the parmesan cheese.
7. Bake at 350°F for 25–30 minutes until the cheese is melted and bubbly.

Notes

Heavy-duty mayonnaise holds up better in this dish and will give you a firmer filling.

Make sure you take the time to drain the tomatoes well, otherwise your pie could be runny.

Ingredients

- 2 fresh or frozen deep-dish pie shells, cooked and cooled
- 3 tomatoes
- Oven-Roasted Vegetables (see recipe below)
- 2 tsp. salt
- 1½ cups heavy-duty mayonnaise
- ½ cup apple cider vinegar
- 1 tsp. granulated garlic
- 4 cups fresh shredded cheese of your choice
- Salt and pepper to taste
- Parmesan cheese

Oven-Roasted Vegetables

Makes 6 cups (enough for 2 pies)

Roasted vegetables are a delicious alternative to steamed vegetables. The roasting really brings out their natural sweetness and better preserves their nutritional value. The slight char and crispy edges make for a beautiful bowl and often make them more desirable to picky vegetable eaters.

Instructions

1. Preheat the oven to 450°F.
2. Line a baking sheet with parchment paper. You may need to use two baking sheets to avoid crowding the vegetables while they roast.
3. Spread the vegetables on the pan and drizzle them with the olive oil.
4. Sprinkle the vegetables with salt, pepper, and garlic. Mix with your hands until all the vegetables are coated.
5. Bake for 20 minutes, then rotate the pan and bake for 10 minutes more until they are light brown and tender.

Ingredients

- 1 large red onion, sliced
- 1 broccoli crown, cut into bite-sized pieces
- 1 medium sweet potato, peeled and sliced thin
- 1 large red pepper, cut into strips
- 2 large carrots, peeled and cut into thin rounds
- 8–10 Brussels sprouts, sliced thin
- 5–6 Tbsp. olive oil
- 2 tsp. granulated garlic
- 1–2 tsp. kosher salt
- 1 tsp. black pepper

Tomato Pie

Makes 2 pies

Tomato pie is as Southern as summer, fireflies, and sweet tea. When the spring tomatoes are ruby red, we start cranking out tomato pies at the café. Our customers eat them as fast as we can make them.

Ingredients

- 2 fresh or frozen deep-dish pie shells, cooked and cooled
- 4–5 tomatoes
- 1 sweet Vidalia onion, sliced and lightly sautéed
- 2 tsp. salt
- 1½ cups heavy-duty mayonnaise
- ½ cup apple cider vinegar
- 1 tsp. granulated garlic
- 4 cups fresh shredded cheese of your choice
- Salt and pepper to taste
- Chopped fresh basil

Instructions

1. Slice the tomatoes thin and lay them in a large colander. Salt them well and let them drain into the sink for an hour. After they've drained, place them on paper towels and pat them dry.
2. Mix the mayonnaise, vinegar, garlic, cheeses, salt, and pepper.
3. Put a layer of tomatoes in the pie shell.
4. Top the layer of tomatoes with part of the mayonnaise and cheese mixture, and add a layer of sautéed onions.
5. Add another layer of tomatoes and finish with the mayonnaise and cheese mixture.
6. Lay a few tomatoes and basil leaves on top.
7. Bake at 350°F for 25–30 minutes until the cheese is melted and bubbly.

Notes

Use a variety of tomatoes if they are available.

Heavy-duty mayonnaise holds up better in this dish and will give you a firmer filling.

Make sure you take the time to drain the tomatoes well, otherwise your pie could be runny.

Use a mixture of cheese that you love. I often use part smoked cheese and part mozzarella.

Experiment with herbs too. Try rosemary, oregano, or thyme.

Savory Burger Stack

Makes 6 servings

This is one of those meals that you can either intentionally put together or build from leftovers. I love it when it works that way!

Instructions

1. Prepare the mashed potatoes according to the recipe, adding shredded white cheddar before serving. If you are using leftover mashed potatoes, add the shredded cheddar prior to warming them up.

2. Prepare the gravy according to the recipe and set it aside.

3. Place the ground beef in a bowl and season it with paprika, salt, pepper, brown sugar, garlic powder, and onion powder. Mix it well with your hands.

4. Shape the mixture into six patties.

5. In a skillet, or on your grill, cook the patties until they reach the desired internal temperature. Remove them from the heat and set them aside.

6. In a large pan on medium heat, fry the eggs, leaving the yolk soft. Turn the heat off and set them aside.

7. On a large plate or in a deep dish, place a scoop of the cheesy potatoes, add a ground beef patty, top with an egg (being careful to not disturb the yolk), and finish with gravy, shredded cheese, and chopped parsley. You can also add chopped tomatoes, pickled onions, or peppers.

Notes

You can use brown gravy or white gravy for this dish.

You do not have to be married to the cheese I use in the recipe—try the variety you love the most.

Ingredients

- Mashed Potatoes (see page 69)
- 1½–2 cups shredded white cheddar cheese
- Shredded Colby cheese
- 6 eggs
- 2 lbs. ground beef
- 1½ tsp. paprika
- 1 tsp. salt
- 1 tsp. pepper
- ½ tsp. brown sugar
- ½ tsp. garlic powder
- ¼ tsp. onion powder
- Gravy

Sunday Pot Roast

Makes 8 servings

This pot roast is one of the first dishes that comes to mind when someone talks about comfort food. It's the Sunday dish prepared by mothers and grandmothers everywhere. If my family wasn't making sandwiches with the leftovers, my mom would chop the roast and the vegetables up and make hash for us. So yummy!

Instructions

1. Preheat the oven to 350°F.
2. Add the oil to a large Dutch oven over medium-high heat.
3. Season each side of the roast with salt and pepper and place it in the hot oil. Sear it on every side for 3–4 minutes until browned. Remove the roast from the pan and set it aside.
4. Add the garlic to the pot and sauté for 1 minute. Add the beef broth and beer and deglaze the pan. Add the roast back to the pot.
5. Drizzle the Worcestershire sauce and liquid smoke over the roast. Place the vegetables in the pot around and on top of the roast.
6. Put a lid or foil cover on the pot. Cook for 3–3½ hours or until the internal temperature is 205°F and the meat shreds easily with a fork. Make sure that your vegetables are tender too.
7. Plate your roast with the vegetables and enjoy.

Ingredients

- 5-lb. chuck or round roast
- 2 tsp. salt
- 1 tsp. black pepper
- 3 Tbsp. vegetable oil
- 4 garlic cloves, minced
- 2 cups beef broth
- 12 oz. beer
- ¼ cup Worcestershire sauce
- 2 Tbsp. liquid smoke
- 3 white or sweet onions
- 1 lb. carrots, cleaned and cut into chunks
- 2 lbs. red or Yukon Gold potatoes, cut into chunks
- 1 medium white onion, chopped
- 1 clove garlic, minced
- ½ cup flour
- 1 tsp. salt
- 2 cups chicken broth

Notes

Your sear will be best if you let your roast come to room temperature and pat it dry with a paper towel prior to seasoning it.

My favorite roast to use is a chuck roast, which always falls apart when it's finished. If you want a better slicing roast, you can use a round roast.

You can also prepare this in a slow cooker by searing your roast and placing it with all the remaining ingredients in the pot and cooking on low for 8 hours.

Cubed Steaks with Mushroom Gravy

Makes 4 servings

When I have a deep yearning for something that comforts like a warm blanket on a rainy day, I reach for this recipe. The deep and rich flavor of the mushrooms complements the cubed steaks.

Instructions

1. Using paper towels, dry both sides of the steaks, then let them rest at room temperature for an hour.
2. Combine the flour, seasoned salt, and pepper in a bowl.
3. Put the buttermilk in a second bowl.
4. In a large skillet, add 2 Tbsp. of oil and heat over medium-high heat.
5. Dredge the steaks in buttermilk, then coat them in flour. Place them in the skillet and cook one side until it's browned, then flip and cook the other side. For four steaks, you might have to work in two batches. While the second batch is cooking, I keep the others warm in an oven set to 250°F. Also, do not remove the bits left in the bottom of the pan—you will need them.
6. When the steaks are done, add the butter to the skillet, then add the onions and mushrooms and cook until tender. While they are cooking, use a spatula to scrape up and incorporate the bits off the bottom of the pan.
7. When the onions and mushrooms are soft, add the sour cream and mix well. Taste and season as desired.
8. When serving, plate one steak and smother it with the mushroom and onion gravy.

Ingredients

- 4 cubed steaks
- 2 cups flour
- 2 tsp. seasoned salt
- 1 tsp. pepper
- 1 cup buttermilk
- Oil for frying
- 2 Tbsp. butter
- 2 large white onions, sliced into rings
- 1 lb. mushrooms, cleaned and sliced
- 2 cups sour cream
- Salt and pepper, to taste

Notes

Do not crowd your steaks when cooking, I suggest sticking to two at a time. Overcrowding can lead to overcooking which leads to tough steaks.

Did you know that there are approximately 14,000 varieties of mushrooms? Caution—they are not all edible!

Mushrooms have health benefits: they are a major source of vitamin D, support a healthy immune system, and protect brain health, to name a few.

Open-Faced Sloppy Joes

Makes 12 servings

A great sloppy joe is nostalgic and takes us back to a simpler time and place. Pairing it up with a Southern-staple-turned-waffle creates an impressive and tasty, yet simple meal.

Instructions

1. In a large skillet, add the ground beef and brown it over medium-high heat. Drain off the fat.
2. Add the onions, red or green bell pepper if using, and garlic. Cook until the onions get soft.
3. Add the remaining ingredients and mix well. Turn the heat to medium-low and continue to cook and simmer for about an hour.
4. Put about a ¼–⅓ cup of the mixture on top of each waffle piece and top with pickled red onions, a pickle slice, and a sprinkle of chili pepper blend.

Notes

If you like your joes a little sweeter, add more brown sugar.

If you like them spicier, add chili pepper blend while the mixture is simmering.

Ingredients

- 2½ lbs. ground beef
- 1 medium sweet yellow onion, diced
- 4 cloves garlic, minced
- 2 cups ketchup
- ½ cup water
- 2 Tbsp. brown sugar
- 1 tsp. dry mustard
- 2 tsp. chili powder
- 1 Tbsp. Worcestershire sauce
- 4 Tbsp. tomato paste
- ½ green or red bell pepper, diced, optional
- Cornbread Waffles (see recipe below)
- Pickled Red Onions (see page 53), pickle slices, and chili pepper blend, I use Olde Virden's Red Hot Sprinkle

Cornbread Waffles

Makes 8 servings

Sometimes we need something more than bread, buns, or bowls for our dinner. Be it sweet or savory, waffles, with their deep little crevasses, hold onto whatever you choose to top them with. Try toppings such as chili, eggs, pimento cheese, pulled pork, and so much more!

Instructions

1. Mix all the ingredients together in a bowl and stir gently to incorporate.
2. Heat your waffle iron until the ready-to-use light comes on. For this recipe I used a Belgian waffle iron.
3. Put the cornbread batter into the waffle iron and cook until done.
4. When the waffles come out, top each piece with a slice of cheddar cheese.

Ingredients

- 2½ cups self-rising yellow cornmeal
- 2 cups buttermilk
- ⅓ cup melted shortening, I use Crisco
- 2 eggs, beaten
- ¼ cup sugar
- 1½ tsp. kosher salt
- One 15.25-oz. can corn, partially drained

Notes

Cornbread waffles are also delicious topped with eggs and bacon, chicken, macaroni and cheese, or chili.

Down-Home Goulash

Makes 10 servings

This is a sure-fire comfort food favorite. Haven't we all been seated around the family dinner table with a big bowl of steamy goulash being passed around, waiting anxiously for our turn? This is basic goodness, so there's no need to "fancy it up" with extra seasoning. With that said, I always was and still am a ketchup fanatic. I do stir some into my goulash (and my chili, sloppy joes, beef stew, and chili beans and rice). It always drove my parents crazy, and still does!

Ingredients

- 1 Tbsp. oil
- 1 medium white or yellow onion, diced
- 2 lbs. ground beef
- 2 Tbsp. granulated garlic
- One 10-oz. can tomatoes and green chilies, I use Ro-Tel
- Two 15-oz. cans tomato sauce
- 2 Tbsp. Worcestershire sauce
- Salt, to taste
- 16 oz. elbow macaroni

Instructions

1. In a large pot, bring water to boil and cook the macaroni as instructed. Drain and set aside.
2. In the same large pot on medium-high heat, add the oil, onions, and ground beef. Cook until the beef is brown and the onions are soft. Add the garlic and cook for one minute.
3. Stir in the tomatoes and green chilies, tomato sauce, Worcestershire sauce, cooked noodles, and salt.
4. You are ready to serve.

Notes

Try adding shredded cheese, red pepper flakes, green peppers, or Italian seasoning.

My family always had broiled toast with ours. My mom took bread, put three pats of butter on top, and broiled it in the oven until the butter melted and the edges were toasty brown.

You can use other noodle shapes if you like, but you'll be messing with history—do you really want to do that?

Spicy Smoked Pimento Cheese

Makes 12 servings

It was not until I moved to Tennessee that I was formally introduced to pimento cheese. My first thought was, "What in the heck is that?" Being the cheese lover that I am, I was game to try it. Wow, how perfectly delicious it was! As I usually do, I experimented with recipes, creating as many variations as I could. This is one of my very favorites.

Instructions

1. Place all the shredded cheese into a large bowl.
2. Add the remaining ingredients and mix until everything is combined. I usually put on a pair of gloves and mix by hand. It's much easier than trying to use a handheld mixer.
3. Refrigerate and enjoy!

Ingredients

- 1 lb. pepper jack, shredded
- 1 lb. sharp cheddar, shredded
- ½ lb. smoked gouda, shredded
- 4 cups heavy-duty mayonnaise
- 1 cup sour cream
- Salt and pepper
- 1 cup roasted red peppers, chopped
- ¼–½ cup pickled jalapeños, chopped
- 3 Tbsp. jalapeño juice
- 1 Tbsp. granulated garlic
- 1½ Tbsp. chili pepper blend, I use Olde Virden's Red Hot Sprinkle
- 3–4 Tbsp. smoked paprika
- One 4-oz. can diced green chiles, drained

Notes

Do your tastebuds a favor and shred your own cheese instead of using preshredded.

This has been a Southern staple for over 50 years. It is often referred to as Carolina Caviar or Southern Pâté.

Pimento cheese can be served cold as a dip or a spread, on grilled cheese sandwiches, added into pasta, or as a filling for deviled eggs or celery.

BBQ Pizza

Chef Chris Grove, Certified Food Judge for the World Food Championships and BBQ Cookbook Author

Makes 1 large pizza

You can't go wrong when combining two classic comfort foods like BBQ and pizza. We slow smoke our own pork BBQ, but there is no shame in buying BBQ from your local BBQ joint or buying a ball of pizza dough from a pizza shop or select grocery stores. Instead of a tomato-based pizza sauce, our BBQ pizza features a smoked cheddar cheese sauce perfect for BBQ.

Instructions

1. Preheat your oven or a grill set up for indirect heat to 500°F.

2. Melt the butter over medium heat in a medium saucepot and whisk in the flour until ingredients are combined and fragrant, about 2–3 minutes. While constantly whisking, slowly pour in the milk and continue whisking until it achieves a sauce-like consistency. Bring to a low simmer and add the cheese in batches, waiting each time for the cheese to melt before proceeding. Stir in the seasoning and add salt to taste. Remove from heat.

3. Roll out the pizza dough on a floured surface and poke holes to "dock" the pizza dough using a fork or a docking tool. Brush the crust edges with olive oil. Spread a thin layer of the cheddar sauce onto the pizza dough, excluding the edges. Top with half of the pork and all the onion rings and jalapeño. Top that with mozzarella. Add the remaining pork.

4. Place a pizza stone in the oven or grill and allow it to preheat for 10 minutes. Transfer the pizza to the pizza stone. Cook for 8 minutes. Then rotate the pizza 180 degrees and add the bacon. Drizzle the two barbecue sauces over the pizza. Continue cooking until the crust is golden and the cheese has started to brown, about another 4 minutes.

5. Remove from heat and rest on a cooling rack for 5 minutes. Transfer to a cutting board, slice and serve.

Ingredients

- 5 Tbsp. unsalted butter
- 2 oz. all-purpose flour
- 1½ cups milk
- 2 tsp. smoky barbecue rub
- ½ tsp. kosher salt
- 3 oz. smoked cheddar, shredded
- Pizza crust dough, enough for a 12" pizza
- ½ cup chopped smoked pork
- 2 red onion slices
- 1 jalapeño, cored and sliced
- 4 oz. mozzarella cheese, shredded
- 4 pieces bacon, cooked and crumbled
- ⅓ cup golden mustard barbecue sauce
- ⅓ cup sweet barbecue sauce
- 1 Tbsp. olive oil

Cast-Iron Deep-Dish Pizza

Makes 4 servings

First, let me tell you that my favorite food is pizza, and I could eat it every day. I tend to steer toward cracker-type thin and crispy crust, the one that crunches when you bite into it. On occasion, however, I do crave a thick, chewy pan pizza. The type where the cheese sneaks down between the crust and the pan and crisps to a golden brown. My cast-iron pan works great to sear that crispy outer crust and leave it tender and chewy on the inside.

Ingredients

- Pizza crust dough, enough for a 12" pizza
- 2–3 Tbsp. vegetable oil
- 3 cups pizza sauce
- 4 cups mozzarella, shredded
- Toppings, as desired
- Parmesan cheese

Instructions

1. Heat your oven as high as it will go. It will ensure that your crust is crispy outside and chewy inside.
2. Oil your cast-iron skillet. I use a 10" pan.
3. Press your dough into the pan, letting it come up the sides. Pop any air bubbles that you see.
4. Add a layer of sauce and a layer of cheese. Repeat.
5. Add your chosen toppings and sprinkle with a handful of mozzarella cheese.
6. Bake for 12–15 minutes or until the top is golden brown and bubbly and the bottom of the crust is brown and crisp. Check this by lifting the edge of your pizza with a thin spatula.
7. When your pizza is done, sprinkle with parmesan cheese.
8. Slice and enjoy!

Notes

Make your own pizza crust, buy it from a local pizzeria, or find it in the deli section of most supermarkets.

Pepperoni is America's favorite pizza topping.

Americans eat about 350 slices of pizza per second!

October is National Pizza Month.

Candied Jalapeño Mac and Cheese

Makes 8 servings

If you enjoy a little kick in your mac and cheese, this is the one for you.

Ingredients

- 16 oz. gemelli pasta
- 6 Tbsp. butter
- 6 Tbsp. flour
- 3 cups whole milk
- 1 cup half-and-half
- 1 tsp. salt
- ½ tsp. pepper
- 1 cup candied jalapeño slices
- ½ cup diced candied jalapeño pieces
- 1 cup shredded white cheddar cheese
- 1 cup shredded pepper jack cheese
- Green onion and grated parmesan cheese for garnish

Instructions

1. Cook the pasta according to package directions, drain, and set it aside.
2. Make a roux by putting the butter and flour in a medium pot and cooking on medium heat until the butter melts and the mixture starts to bubble, making sure to whisk to avoid burning. Cook for one minute.
3. Slowly whisk in the milk and half-and-half. Let the mixture come to a simmer and keep whisking until it thickens like gravy.
4. Add the salt and pepper. Remove from the heat and set aside.
5. Slowly add the shredded cheese to the roux and stir until it melts and is creamy.
6. Add the jalapeño slices and the diced pieces, then add the pasta and mix well.
7. Garnish with green onion and grated parmesan cheese. Serve hot and enjoy!

Notes

Use whatever shape of pasta you have on hand, or whatever your favorite is.

Candied jalapeños are a sweet and spicy jalapeño cooked in a sugary syrup. They are sometimes referred to as Cowboy Candy.

You can eliminate the pepper jack and use two cups of cheddar if you are concerned about the heat level.

A "roux" is a cooked mixture of flour and fat (butter in this recipe) used to thicken soups and sauces.

Beer Cheese Mac and Cheese

Makes 8 servings

Beer cheese mac and cheese is rich and bold—heaven in a bowl. For a real treat, serve this with warm soft pretzels.

Instructions

1. Cook the pasta according to the package directions, drain and set aside.
2. Make a roux by putting the butter and flour in a medium pot and cooking on medium heat until the butter melts and the mixture starts to bubble, making sure to whisk to avoid burning. Cook for 1 minute.
3. Slowly whisk in the milk, then add the beer and whisk. Let the mixture come to a simmer.
4. Add the salt, pepper, paprika, garlic, and dried mustard, then mix well. Remove from the heat and set aside.
5. Slowly add the shredded cheese and stir until it melts and is creamy.
6. Add the pasta and mix well.
7. Garnish with green onion and Red Hot Sprinkle. Serve hot and enjoy!

Ingredients

- 16 oz. rigatoni pasta
- 4 Tbsp. butter
- 6 Tbsp. flour
- 2 cups whole milk
- 1 cup beer of your choice
- 1 tsp. salt
- ½ tsp. pepper
- ½ tsp. paprika
- ½ tsp. garlic
- ½ tsp. dried mustard
- 2 cups shredded sharp cheddar
- 1 cup shredded Gruyère
- Green onions and chili pepper blend, I use Old Virden's Red Hot Sprinkle, to garnish

Notes

I like to use pasta shapes that have nooks and crannies that will "trap" the cheese. Anything with ridges, hollow centers, or corkscrews will hang on to that cheesy goodness.

Some of the best cheeses to use for mac and cheese are those that melt well, such as sharp cheddar, Gruyère, cream cheese, gouda, and the extra-tangy goat cheese. If you can find sharp cheddar with peppers in it, you can make a great sauce.

The darker the beer you use in this recipe, the more beer flavor your sauce will have.

Pizza Mac and Cheese

Makes 8 servings

What? Two of the most comforting foods known to humankind in one savory, creamy bowl of heaven? I say yes, yes, a million times yes.

Ingredients

- 16 oz. cheese mini ravioli
- 6–8 oz. sliced pepperoni
- 1 cup pizza sauce
- 6 Tbsp. butter
- 6 Tbsp. flour
- 3 cups whole milk
- 1 cup half-and-half
- 1 tsp. salt
- ½ tsp. pepper
- 1 tsp. chili pepper blend, I use Olde Virden's Red Hot Sprinkle
- 2 cups shredded cheddar cheese
- Parsley and grated parmesan, for garnish

Instructions

1. Cook the ravioli according to the package directions, drain and set aside.
2. Slice the pepperoni into strips and fry in a small saucepan until lightly crisped. Drain them on a paper towel and set aside.
3. Make a roux by putting the butter and flour in a medium pot and cooking on medium heat until the butter melts and the mixture starts to bubble, making sure to whisk to avoid burning. Cook for 1 minute.
4. Slowly whisk in the milk and half-and-half. Let the mixture come to a simmer and keep whisking until it thickens like gravy.
5. Add the salt, pepper, chili pepper blend, and pizza sauce. Remove from the heat and set aside.
6. Slowly add the shredded cheese to the roux and stir until it melts and is completely incorporated and creamy.
7. Add the pepperoni and the ravioli and mix well.
8. Garnish with parsley and grated parmesan cheese. Serve hot and enjoy!

Notes

Try adding other pizza elements, too, such as onions, peppers, or olives.

According to a July 2022 issue of *Reader's Digest*, pizza and mac and cheese are among the most popular foods in America.

For the creamiest mac and cheese, warm your milk before adding it to your flour and butter roux.

Pan-Seared Hot Honey Balsamic Chicken Thighs

Makes 6 servings

I love using my cast-iron skillet. It reminds me of all the warm comforting meals that my grandmother made us in her cast iron. These chicken thighs are no exception. The dish presents well and provides as much comfort as it does beauty.

Ingredients

- 2–3 lbs. skin-on, bone-in chicken thighs
- Salt and pepper
- 1 Tbsp. olive oil
- 1 Tbsp. butter
- ½ cup balsamic vinegar
- ¼ cup hot honey
- 1–2 pts. mixed grape or cherry tomatoes, yellow and red
- 3–4 fresh rosemary sprigs

Notes

To cut the heat, use plain honey instead of hot honey.

Rosemary naturally complements chicken.

Instructions

1. In a large cast-iron skillet on medium heat, melt the butter and olive oil.
2. Pat each of the chicken thighs dry with paper towels and season them with salt and pepper.
3. In a small bowl, mix the balsamic vinegar and hot honey until fully incorporated.
4. Place the thighs in a hot skillet, skin side down for 9–10 minutes, then turn them and brown the other side.
5. When the second side has browned, turn the heat to medium-low, add the balsamic vinegar and hot honey mixture over the tops of the thighs, and let them cook.
6. Place your tomatoes throughout the pan, letting the heat sear them.
7. When the internal temperature of the chicken reaches 165°F, remove the skillet from the heat and place sprigs of fresh rosemary throughout the pan while the chicken rests.
8. Serve in the cast-iron skillet.

Skillet-Roasted Chicken

Chef Chris Grove, Certified Food Judge for the World Food Championships and BBQ Cookbook Author

Makes 4 servings

Skillet roasting a chicken is easy and provides a striking presentation. It involves the "spatchcocking" technique, which is a butchering technique that you can do yourself or have a full-service butcher do for you. I like to take it to the next level and fire-roast the chicken on the grill, but this also works well in the oven.

Ingredients
- 4-lb. whole chicken
- 1 Tbsp. high-temperature cooking oil such as peanut, avocado, or canola oil
- 1 Tbsp. all-purpose seasoning, I used Morton's Season-All Seasoned Salt
- 2 tsp. smoked paprika
- 1 tsp. ground black pepper
- 1 tsp. Italian seasoning
- 2 stalks celery, cut into 3" pieces
- 4–6 cloves garlic, peeled
- ½ cup chicken stock

Instructions

1. Spatchcock and air-dry the bird. Place the chicken breast side down. Use a pair of poultry shears to cut along each side of the backbone and remove it. Flip the chicken, place the heel of a hand on the center of the chicken breast (think chicken CPR), and press firmly down to flatten the chicken. You will hear cracking, don't panic. Tuck the wing tips behind the chicken. Place the spatchcocked chicken on a tray in the refrigerator and let it air dry for an hour. Drying will provide a crispy crust.

2. Season the chicken. Pat the chicken dry (if not air-dried) and lightly coat the chicken with 1 Tbsp. of cooking oil. Mix the rub and season the chicken evenly.

3. Preheat an oven or a grill set up for indirect heat to 425°F. Place the chicken cut side down in a 12-inch skillet and place in the oven. Cook for 45 minutes, and then add the garlic and celery to the skillet. Finish cooking until the skin is golden, crispy, and the internal temperature of the chicken breast is 160°F, a total cook time of 1 hour.

4. Rest the chicken. Remove the skillet from heat and temporarily set the chicken aside. Add the stock to the skillet and stir, scraping up the chicken drippings. Return the chicken to the skillet and allow it to rest for 5 to 10 minutes.

5. Serve the chicken. Use a carving knife to remove each breast from the chicken and slice them sideways. Cut the chicken's wings, thighs, and legs and pull any loose white meat from the chest cavity. Drizzle the pan drippings over the prepared chicken pieces and serve.

TIP:
To spatchcock or butterfly your chicken, remove the backbone using sharp kitchen shears and flatten the chicken so that the meat can more evenly roast.

CHAPTER 8

Delectable Desserts

My family is all about "just a little something sweet" after dinner. And before bed, and all points in between! The recipes in this section are our favorites—the tried and tested treats that are well worth the calories!

page 103

page 106

page 117

page 110

page 107

Rhubarb Cake

Makes 12 servings

Rhubarb was plentiful in the Midwest where I grew up, and it seemed like my mom and Grandmother were always cooking with it. We had jams, pies, sauces, and desserts. I wasn't much of a fan, I must admit. In the South, it's not an ingredient that we see as much since Southern heat is not conducive to a crop of healthy rhubarb. This one's a nod to my northern friends!

Ingredients

- ½ cup shortening
- 1½ cups sugar
- 2 eggs
- 1 cup buttermilk
- 1¾ cups flour
- 1 tsp. baking soda
- ½ tsp. salt
- 2 cups fresh or frozen rhubarb
- ¼ cup sugar
- 2 tsp. cinnamon

Instructions

1. Preheat the oven to 325°F.
2. Grease a 9" x 13" pan.
3. Cream together the sugar and shortening, then add the eggs and beat well.
4. Add the buttermilk alternately with the flour, baking soda, and salt.
5. Fold in the rhubarb and sprinkle the top with the sugar and cinnamon.
6. Bake for 50–55 minutes.

Notes

Serve with fresh whipped cream or ice cream on the side—this is a very moist cake.

Rhubarb is naturally low in cholesterol and sodium and offers a good source of fiber, vitamins C and K, calcium, and potassium.

1 lb. of fresh rhubarb yields 2½–3 cups of chopped rhubarb pieces. The redder the stalk, the sweeter the flavor.

The leaves are poisonous, so be sure to discard them.

Momma Kim's Chocolate Chip Cookies

Makes about 3 dozen cookies

There is something about a batch of chocolate chip cookies fresh out of the oven that warms your heart. When the aroma from the oven fills the house, it makes you feel like a kid again. I have been making these for my friends and family for years to mend broken hearts, to celebrate accomplishments, or just because. These are a bit crunchy on the outside and gooey and soft on the inside, just the way we like them.

Ingredients

- 2¼ cups all-purpose flour
- 1 tsp. baking soda
- ¾ tsp. kosher salt
- 1 stick soft butter
- ½ cup shortening
- ¾ cup granulated sugar
- ¾ cup packed light brown sugar
- 1 tsp. vanilla
- 2 eggs, room temperature
- 18 oz. chocolate chips mixed, I use a mix of milk chocolate, dark chocolate, and semisweet
- Sea salt flakes, optional

Instructions

1. Preheat your oven to 375°F.
2. In a bowl, mix the flour, baking soda, and salt. Set aside.
3. In a separate large bowl, or in a stand mixer, beat the butter, shortening, sugars, and vanilla together until creamy. Add the eggs and mix well.
4. Gradually add the flour mixture, making sure to mix well between additions.
5. Stir in the chocolate chips.
6. Drop tablespoon-size balls of dough on an ungreased cookie sheet and bake for 11–12 minutes until the cookies are lightly brown on the edges.
7. While they are still on the pan, I add a sprinkle of sea salt flakes on top. This is optional.
8. Let them cool slightly on the pan, then move them to a wire rack to completely cool.

Notes

Use any combination of chocolate chips that you like. If I can find them, I often add espresso chocolate chips, too!

This recipe will yield more cookies if you want to make the dough balls smaller. Make sure you adjust your cooking time accordingly.

Pineapple Chiffon Pie

Makes 12 servings

Doesn't the name of this pie sound sweet, fluffy, and decadent? It's the perfect name for a perfect pie.

Ingredients

- 9 oz. crushed pineapple in syrup
- 3 oz. lemon Jell-O
- 8 oz. cream cheese, room temperature
- ¾ cup sugar
- 1 cup evaporated milk
- 2 Tbsp. lemon juice
- Prebaked pie shell
- Whipped cream, for serving

Instructions

1. Put the evaporated milk in a small bowl and place it in the freezer. Keep it in there until it is almost frozen.
2. Drain the pineapple and save the syrup.
3. In a measuring cup, add the syrup and enough water to make 1 cup, then place the mixture in a saucepan and heat to boiling. Remove it from the heat and stir in the Jell-O until it is dissolved.
4. In a large bowl, beat the cream cheese, sugar, and pineapple together until creamy.
5. At low speed, slowly add in the gelatin mixture and blend until well mixed.
6. Chill until the mixture has thickened.
7. Take the cold evaporated milk and beat it until it is fluffy. Add the lemon juice and beat again until stiff peaks form.
8. Add this to the thickened gelatin mixture and fold until well blended.
9. Put in a prebaked pie shell.
10. Refrigerate and serve with whipped cream.

Notes

The pineapple is the ultimate symbol of Southern hospitality.

Hawaii produces a third of all the pineapples in the world.

Pineapple is the most debated and controversial pizza topping.

Whiskey Truffles

Makes 12 servings

We have friends who invited us to a dinner party, and they just so happen to be whiskey lovers. We were asked to bring a dessert, so I found my truffle recipe and added a bit of spirit to it! Rich, delicious, and decadent—these are the perfect indulgent treat.

Instructions

1. Put chocolate, heavy cream, and butter in a microwave-safe bowl.
2. Heat until the chocolate is melted and smooth. Do this is in short intervals so that you do not burn the chocolate.
3. Stir in the whiskey and sea salt, and mix well.
4. Refrigerate the mixture until it is chilled. This may take up to 3 hours.
5. Use a small scoop to shape the truffles into the desired size.
6. Roll the truffles in cocoa powder, sprinkles, nuts, or granulated honey, if desired.
7. Keep them refrigerated until you are ready to serve.

Notes

Use your favorite whiskey for this treat.

For an interesting flavor twist, substitute a smoked salt for the sea salt in the recipe.

Whiskey and chocolate pair together well because their flavor profiles are quite similar.

Ingredients

- 1 lb. high quality dark chocolate, chopped into small pieces
- ⅓ cup heavy cream
- 2 Tbsp. butter
- ⅓ cup whiskey
- 1 tsp. sea salt
- Unsweetened cocoa powder, chopped roasted nuts, chocolate sprinkles, or granulated honey, optional for rolling the finished truffles in

Toasted Coconut Pudding

Makes 10 servings

If you are a coconut lover, this recipe is for you. This is a cross between creamy pudding and a perfectly toasted coconut. One bite is all it takes to be hooked.

Ingredients

- Two 14-oz. bags shredded sweetened coconut
- Two 3.4-oz. boxes instant coconut pudding
- 2 cups whole milk
- 1½ cups heavy cream
- 14 oz. sweetened condensed milk
- ⅓ cup powdered sugar
- 1 tsp. vanilla extract
- 1 tsp. coconut extract
- Whipped cream and vanilla wafers, optional, for serving

Instructions

1. Preheat the oven to 425°F. Lay parchment paper on a cookie sheet and spread the coconut out in an even layer. You may need two cookie sheets.
2. Bake for about 6–8 minutes total, ensuring that all the coconut is evenly browned a crispy. Halfway through baking, stir it with a spoon. When brown, remove it from the oven and let it cool.
3. In a large mixing bowl, add the pudding mix, milk, and condensed milk and mix until smooth. Set aside for 5 minutes.
4. In another large, chilled mixing bowl beat the heavy cream, powdered sugar, and extracts until stiff peaks form.
5. Gently fold the whipped cream mixture into the pudding mixture until smooth.
6. Stir in half of the toasted coconut.
7. Cover and refrigerate for 2 hours before serving.
8. To serve, put the pudding in bowls and garnish with toasted coconut and whipped cream. You can also add vanilla wafers if you like.

Notes

Anytime you are whipping heavy cream to stiff peaks, prechill your bowl and beaters in the refrigerator for 30 minutes.

Did you know workers can harvest up to 180 coconuts from a single coconut tree in one season? That's a lot of pudding!

Cranberry Carrot Cake

Makes 10–12 servings

Good carrot cake is one of my top three favorite desserts. It must be moist, full of flavor and packed full of carrots, pineapple, and raisins (nuts optional). I've made this cake more of a fall recipe with the addition of dried cranberries. Now that I think about it, I'm certain with all the fruit in here, this dessert must actually be healthy!

Instructions

1. Preheat the oven to 350°F. Use pan spray on either a bundt pan, two 9" round pans, or a 9" x 13" pan.
2. Cream together the oil and sugar until mixed well. Add the eggs and the baby food, then mix well.
3. Add the dry ingredients and gently mix.
4. Stir in the pineapple, cranberries, orange zest, and nuts, if using. The batter will be thin, so do not be alarmed.
5. Bake for 30–35 minutes until a toothpick comes out clean. Cool on a wire rack.
6. Frost with Cream Cheese Icing as desired.

Notes

Did you know that George Washington served carrot cake at parties?

In the Middle Ages, sugar was scarce, and carrots were used to sweeten cakes.

Ingredients

- 1¼ cups vegetable oil
- 2 cups of sugar
- 4 eggs, at room temperature
- 2 large jars carrot baby food, enough to equal 14 oz.
- 2 cups of flour
- 2 tsp. baking soda
- 1 tsp. salt
- 1¼ tsp. cinnamon
- 3 large carrots, shredded
- Half 20-oz. can drained, crushed pineapple
- 1 cup dried cranberries
- Zest of one small orange
- 1 cup nuts, optional
- Cream Cheese Icing, recipe below

Cream Cheese Icing

Makes 4 cups

A perfectly balanced cream cheese icing tricks you into thinking you are eating cheesecake. It's a silky, slightly tangy frosting that complements cookies, cakes, muffins, and more.

Instructions

1. Mix the cream cheese and butter until smooth and creamy.
2. Mix in the vanilla, orange zest, and salt until blended.
3. Add the powdered sugar 2 cups at a time, mixing well between additions. Start with 6 cups of powdered sugar and if you think the icing is too thin, add more until your desired consistency is achieved.

Ingredients

- Three 8-oz. blocks cream cheese, room temperature
- 1 cup butter, room temperature
- 1–2 Tbsp. orange zest
- 1 Tbsp. vanilla
- ½ tsp. kosher salt
- 6–7 cups powdered sugar
- Heavy cream, if needed to thin frosting

Notes

For a taste bump, add cinnamon to your cream cheese icing.

If your icing is too thick, add heavy cream or milk a few teaspoons at a time to thin it.

Rice Pudding
Makes 8 servings

This is how we were meant to eat rice! It's classic, creamy, and not too sweet.

Instructions

1. Add the rice, 3 cups of the milk, sugar, and salt in a medium saucepan. Mix them well and stir over medium heat for 30 minutes.

2. In a small bowl, mix the remaining cup of milk and the 4 egg yolks well. Then add to the above mixture.

3. Cook slow and stir frequently until the mixture thickens. If adding raisins or cinnamon, add them now.

4. Pour the mixture into a serving bowl and let it come to room temperature. You can serve this warm or cold. If serving cold, try topping it with a sprinkle of cinnamon or with berry compote and whipped cream.

Notes

It is perfectly ok to have this for breakfast since it's full of dairy!

August 9 is National Rice Pudding Day.

Rice pudding offers more health benefits than other desserts, such as custard or ice cream.

Ingredients

- 3 cups cooked white rice
- 4 cups whole milk, divided
- 1 cup sugar
- 1 tsp. salt
- 4 large egg yolks
- Raisins, optional
- Cinnamon, optional
- Fresh fruit compote, optional

Jen's Berry Shortcake

Makes 12 servings

This is my daughter Jen's favorite dessert. It's my take on strawberry shortcake, amped up a little. I love to incorporate all the fresh summer berries in this dessert. It not only delights your tastebuds, but it's also a colorful eye-catching dessert that brings everyone to the table. I've always used Bisquick to make my shortbread. When Jen was younger, she always asked me to make "BisQuit." So, this is our family's "BisQuit" dessert.

Ingredients

- 3 qts. of mixed berries (sliced strawberries, blackberries, blueberries, and raspberries)
- 1 cup sugar
- 5 cups Original Bisquick Pancake & Baking Mix
- 1¼ cups whole milk
- 6½ Tbsp. sugar
- 5 Tbsp. raw sugar (I use Sugar in the Raw)
- 6½ Tbsp. melted butter
- 2 tsp. vanilla
- Homemade whipped cream, fresh berries, and mint, for serving

Notes

If I am serving adults only, I add orange liqueur to my berry mixture.

Mix orange zest into the berry mixture for added flavor.

Extra cakes will keep in an airtight container for up to three days.

Instructions

1. In a large bowl, mix your berries and sugar, then set the mixture aside. You want a high yield of juice from the berries, so it is best to let these marinate in the refrigerator overnight if you can.
2. Preheat the oven to 425°F.
3. In a large mixing bowl, combine the Bisquick, milk, sugar, melted butter, and vanilla. Stir until a dough forms.
4. Drop the dough in ½ cups onto an ungreased cookie sheet, sprinkle each dough ball with the raw sugar, and bake for 12–14 minutes until golden brown and done in the center.
5. When the cakes come out, brush them with melted butter if desired.
6. Split each cake and fill it with the berry mixture, adding a good amount of the juice.
7. Top with homemade whipped cream, fresh berries, and a mint leaf.

Butterscotch Pumpkin Pie

Makes 8 servings

Growing up, my dad always had Butterscotch Discs and butter rum Life Savers in his pockets, as did my grandmother. I remember loving the smell and taste of them. Imagine the sheer joy and excitement I had when I came across this recipe in a box of my grandmother's handwritten recipes. This is my version of her pie, and it's nostalgic, iconic, and delicious.

Ingredients

- 1 cup butterscotch chips
- 1 cup evaporated milk
- 2 cups canned pure pumpkin
- ½ cup sugar
- 1 Tbsp. flour
- ½ tsp. salt
- 1 tsp. cinnamon
- ½ tsp. nutmeg
- ¼ tsp. cloves
- 3 eggs, slightly beaten

Instructions

1. Preheat the oven to 400°F.
2. Combine the butterscotch pieces and evaporated milk in a bowl and melt them in the microwave. You can also place the ingredients in a small saucepan and melt them on the stove top.
3. Stir in the pumpkin, sugar, flour, salt, and spices. Add the sugar and eggs, then mix well.
4. Pour the mixture into an unbaked pie crust and bake for 45–50 min
5. Let the pie cool and serve with whipped cream.

Notes

Did you know that a pumpkin is fruit?

Pumpkin pie ranks as Americas #2 favorite. Move over, apple pie!

The world's largest pumpkin pie weighed in at 3,699 pounds!

2019 was the last year that Brach's Butterscotch Discs were produced, leaving many of us shattered.

Homemade Pie Crust Two Ways

Makes two 8"–9" pies

If you have been in the café and asked me about pies, it is no secret that I do not really make pies—I feel I have yet to master a truly impressive crust. I am going to share two amazing pie crust recipes with you, one from each of my grandmothers. And yes, I have made both of them!

Grandma M's Quick Pie Crust

Ingredients

- ¼ cup butter, room temperature
- 1 cup flour
- 1 Tbsp. sugar
- ½ tsp. salt
- 1 large egg yolk

Instructions

1. Cream the butter and sugar.
2. Add the egg yolk, salt, and flour, and mix well.
3. Press the mixture into a pie pan to about ¼" thick.
4. Prebake at 350°F until golden if you are using the crust for a pudding pie. If you are making a traditional baked pie, add the fruit filling and bake per the pie instructions.

Grandma S's Pie Crust

Ingredients

- 2½ cups flour
- 1 tsp. salt
- 2 Tbsp. sugar
- ¾ cup chilled butter, cut into small cubes
- ½ cup shortening
- 8 Tbsp. ice water
- 1 Tbsp. milk
- 1 large egg yolk

Instructions

1. Mix the flour, sugar, and salt until they are well incorporated. A food processor works well, although Grandma never used one.
2. Add half of the butter and pulse well or use a pastry blender. Add the remaining butter and mix again.
3. Add the shortening in tablespoon portions and pulse or mix by hand. You want to incorporate the butter and shortening until the bits are the size of peas.
4. Add half of the ice water and pulse or mix. Then keep adding the water a tablespoon at a time until the dough starts to hold together. It is ready when the dough looks crumbly and holds together when you pinch it.
5. Divide your dough into two balls, then lightly dust them with flour, wrap them in plastic, and refrigerate for a few hours.
6. Sprinkle flour on a flat work surface and lay your dough ball in the middle. Dust your rolling pin with flour and roll your dough outward, moving around the dough disc.
7. Once you have reached the desired size, fold the dough in half and place it over the pie dish. Then gently unfold it.
8. Bake per the pie instructions.

Notes

A simple egg wash for your crust is one egg yolk beaten with milk and brushed on the pie crust rim or top if you are making a double-crust pie.

You can cut the rolled crust into small circles to make hand pies.

Flourless Chocolate Espresso Cake

Makes 8 servings

I made this for a client that requested a flourless cake. As I played with my recipe, I was able to enhance the flavor by adding coffee to the mix. Coffee and chocolate, you ask? Absolutely. After you make this, cut a slice for yourself, pour a cup of coffee, and enjoy a quiet moment of heaven. You deserve it!

Instructions

1. Preheat the oven to 300°F. Grease and flour a 9" round pan.
2. In a medium glass bowl, melt the butter and all the chocolate pieces in the microwave. Melt it in bursts and stir in between to make sure that the chocolate does not burn.
3. Add the sugar, coffee, and chocolate mixture to a food processor and blend for 2 minutes.
4. Add the eggs one at a time, and blend for 2 minutes until combined.
5. Pour the batter into the pan.
6. Bake in a water bath for 65 minutes. This is a dense cake, and it will not rise.
7. Cool on a wire rack for 20 minutes and refrigerate until the cake is firm.
8. When serving, run a thin knife around the edge and invert the cake out onto your serving plate.
9. Dust the top with cocoa powder or powdered sugar mixed with instant coffee or espresso.

Ingredients

- 3 sticks butter
- 6 oz. chopped semisweet chocolate
- 6 oz. chopped white chocolate
- 4 oz. chopped unsweetened chocolate
- 1½ cups sugar
- 1 Tbsp. instant coffee or espresso
- 9 large eggs, room temperature
- Cocoa powder or powdered sugar mixed with ½ tsp. instant coffee or espresso, for serving

Notes

If your cake does not release from the pan, try dipping the bottom of the pan in warm water.

Serve this with Coffee-Flavored Whipped Cream for a real treat.

Coffee-Flavored Whipped Cream

Makes 8–10 servings

Nothing hits the spot like homemade whipped cream. This takes less time to make than thawing out a container of frozen whipped topping and it's guaranteed to impress.

Ingredients

- 2 cups chilled heavy cream
- ½ cup powdered sugar
- 2–3 tsp. instant coffee

Instructions

1. Add the heavy cream, powdered sugar, and instant coffee to a chilled mixing bowl.
2. Beat until stiff peaks form, about 5 minutes.
3. Store in a covered container in the refrigerator for up to 4 days.

Notes

Use the extra in your coffee or hot chocolate or to top your ice cream!

Taste of Heaven Cake

Makes 10 servings

This is a cake that I was experimenting with—layering chocolate cake, chocolate and white buttercream, and cheesecake. I asked my family and friends to be my taste testers and the overwhelming response was that this tastes like heaven. Thus, the Taste of Heaven Cake was born. This cake can be a time-consuming project if you make each element from scratch. This recipe is the quicker method, but feel free to use your own recipes for each layer to truly personalize your cake. Also feel free to send me a sample!

Ingredients

- 1 box devil's food cake mix
- 1 cup dark chocolate chips
- 1 cup strong brewed coffee, room temperature
- One 9" chilled cheesecake (store-bought or homemade)
- Chocolate frosting (store-bought or homemade)
- Homemade White Buttercream, see recipe on page 121
- Sliced fresh strawberries, optional

Instructions

1. Preheat the oven to 350°F.
2. For the cakes, follow the directions on back of the box, substituting coffee for the water and adding chocolate chips as the last step.
3. Put the cake batter in two 9" pans and bake as directed. Cool the cakes on a wire rack for 15–20 minutes before removing them from the pans.
4. To assemble the cake, lay one of the 9" layers flat and evenly spread 1 cup of white buttercream on top. If desired, add a layer of fresh strawberry slices.
5. Put the whole cheesecake on top of the first layer. Add about 1 cup of chocolate frosting on top.
6. Add the other 9" chocolate cake on top of the second layer.
7. Cover the entire cake with a thin layer of chocolate frosting and refrigerate for an hour.
8. Take the cake out of the refrigerator, frost the entire cake, and decorate as desired.
9. Store the cake in the refrigerator.

Notes

Using coffee in a chocolate cake deepens and enhances the chocolate flavor.

Did you know that the Austrian postal service once had cheesecake-flavored postage stamps?!

Chocolate cake and cheesecake rank among the top ten most popular desserts in America.

Crème Brûlée

Makes 6 servings

If crème brûlée is on the menu, I am ordering it! While I love the traditional vanilla crème brulee with its perfect custard filling, I occasionally enjoy adding fresh fruit zest, extracts, or steeping fruits and fresh herbs in the cream mixture. Don't forget to have your kitchen torch on hand to create the sugary crunch on top.

Ingredients

- 1 qt. heavy cream
- 1 cup sugar, divided
- 6 large egg yolks
- 1 tsp. pure vanilla
- Fine zest of one orange or lemon

Instructions

1. Preheat the oven to 325°F.
2. Put the heavy cream, vanilla, and zest into a medium saucepan over medium-high heat and bring to a boil. Remove from the heat and let the mixture sit for at least 30 minutes. Strain and remove the zest of you like (I leave it in because I like the pop of flavor).
3. In medium bowl, whisk together ½ cup of sugar and the egg yolks until well blended and lighter in color.
4. Add your cream a little at a time, mixing well until all the cream has been incorporated.
5. Put the cream mixture into six 7- to 8-oz. ramekins. Put the ramekins into a large deep roasting pan and pour enough hot water into the pan to come halfway up the sides of the ramekins.
6. Bake 40–45 minutes until the custard is set but still jiggly in the middle.
7. Remove the ramekins from the pan and refrigerate them for at least 3 hours. When you are ready to serve, remove them from the refrigerator and let them sit for 30 minutes prior to adding the sugar top.
8. Spread ½–¾ cup of sugar equally between each ramekin and use a torch to melt the sugar until lightly browned. This will create that signature crispy top.
9. Allow them to sit for a few minutes prior to serving.

Notes

Did you know there are many alternative names for crème brûlée, including burned cream, burnt cream, Trinity cream, and Cambridge burnt cream

France, Spain, and England all claim to be the country where crème brûlée originated.

The largest crème brûlée, weighing in at 1,599.96 lbs., was made in February 2005. I would love to have been there!

Homemade Vanilla Ice Cream Base

Makes 1 quart

This is a basic classic, but also a delicious base for making creative ice creams. It is endlessly customizable—try adding your favorite flavors, fruits, and candy. Let your imagination be your guide.

Ingredients

- 1 cup heavy cream
- 1 cup whole milk
- ½ cup sugar
- Pinch of salt
- 4 large egg yolks
- 2 tsp. pure vanilla

Instructions

1. Place the egg yolks, sugar, and salt in a medium saucepan and whisk until the color changes to a light yellow.

2. In a small saucepan, heat the milk over medium-low heat until it starts to simmer. Do not let it boil and do not stir it.

3. Gradually add the milk to the egg and sugar mixture, making sure to stir constantly.

4. Return the mixture to the heat until it reaches 165°F, but do not let it boil.

5. As soon as it is almost boiling, remove it from the heat, put it in an airtight container in the refrigerator, and let it chill to 65°F.

6. When the mixture has cooled, stir in the heavy cream and vanilla. Pour the mixture into to your ice cream maker and churn according to your machine's instructions.

Notes

New Zealand consumes more ice cream per capita than any other country—an average of 7.5 gallons per person each year.

The US is in second place with 5.5 gallons. Have you ever suffered from brain freeze? Try pressing your tongue against the roof of your mouth!

Chocolate ice cream was invented before vanilla.

Black Cherry and Goat Cheese Ice Cream

Makes 1 quart

At our café, we make our ice cream by hand. We have a one-quart ice cream maker that we use to experiment with small batches before they make their way to the dip cabinet. The inspiration for this came to me while we were enjoying a charcuterie board at another local establishment. The board included goat cheese and black cherry spread. I was tantalized by the mix of perfect sweetness from the cherries and that bit of tartness from the goat cheese.

Ingredients

- Vanilla Ice Cream, recipe on page 116
- One 8-oz. goat cheese log, room temperature, divided
- One 15-oz. can dark sweet cherries, drained and diced into small pieces

Instructions

1. Make the Vanilla Ice Cream recipe on page 116. In step 2, add 5 oz. of goat cheese to the milk and follow the remaining steps as written.
2. When you place your ice cream in the freezer to set, add the cherries to the custard mixture.
3. Once your ice cream is done, transfer it to a large bowl and stir in pea-sized pieces of the remaining goat cheese.
4. Freeze again, scoop, and enjoy!

Wedding Cake Ice Cream

Makes 1 quart

Close your eyes with the first bite and you will think that you are eating a piece of wedding cake.

Ingredients

- Vanilla Ice Cream, recipe on page 116
- 1 cup white cake mix
- 1½ cups Homemade White Buttercream, recipe on page 121
- Sprinkles and sugar crystals, for serving

Instructions

1. Make the Vanilla Ice Cream recipe on page 116. In step 2, add the white cake mix to the milk and follow the remaining steps as written.
2. When your ice cream is done, transfer it into a large bowl and stir in ½ tsp.-sized dollops of buttercream. You don't want them to disappear, just fold it gently so that you get bites of buttercream with each bite of ice cream.

Homemade Triple Chocolate Ice Cream

Makes 1 quart

To be honest, the name says it all.

Ingredients

- Vanilla Ice Cream, recipe on page 116
- ¼ cup unsweetened cocoa powder
- 12 oz. semisweet chocolate chips, divided
- Hot Fudge Dessert Topping, recipe below

Instructions

1. Make the Vanilla Ice Cream recipe on page 116. In step 2, add the cocoa powder to the milk and whisk well. When you remove the mixture from the heat, add 6 oz. of the chocolate chips and follow the remaining steps as written.
2. When you place your ice cream in the freezer to set, add the remaining chocolate chips to the custard mixture.
3. Serve with Hot Fudge Dessert Topping.

Hot Fudge Dessert Topping

Makes 10–12 servings

What is ice cream without a warm fudgy topping? This is a simple recipe for a hot fudge sauce you can prepare in a snap. My aunt always made this for us growing up and now you can keep it on hand to satisfy those late-night comfort cravings.

Ingredients

- One 5.9-oz. package cook-and-serve chocolate pudding
- 2 cups water
- ⅔ cup peanut butter
- ⅔ cup light corn syrup, I use Karo Light Corn Syrup with Vanilla

Instructions

1. Mix the pudding and the water in a medium saucepan over medium-high heat until the mixture comes to a boil.
2. Add the peanut butter and corn syrup. Stir well to incorporate.
3. Serve hot or cold over your favorite ice cream or dessert.
4. Store in the refrigerator.

Notes

The hot fudge sundae was created in 1906 at C.C. Brown, a brand-new ice cream parlor that had just popped up in Los Angeles.

Fun Funfetti Cake

Makes 10–12 servings

Sprinkles in a cake just make you smile. Actually, sprinkles in general just scream happiness, smiles, celebration, and loads of fun. This is a moist, delicious cake you can customize for any celebration (or make just because you really want a cake with sprinkles).

Instructions

1. Preheat the oven to 325°F.
2. Spray three 8" round pans with a nonstick spray and dust them with flour.
3. In a medium bowl, whisk the dry ingredients together.
4. In a large bowl or a stand mixer, beat the butter, oil, and sugar on high speed until fluffy. This will take about 5 minutes.
5. Add the eggs one a time, beating in between at medium speed, making sure they are fully incorporated.
6. Add the sour cream and mix on medium speed for a minute until mixed in.
7. With your mixer on low speed, add the flour 1 cup at a time, followed by half of your buttermilk. Then repeat, making sure the remaining flour is the last addition. Mix until well incorporated.
8. With your mixer still on low speed, add the extract and scrape down the sides of bowl. Gently fold in the sprinkles.
9. Put even amounts of batter in the pans and bake for 25–30 minutes or until a toothpick comes out clean, being careful to not overbake. It's okay if the toothpick comes out with a few crumbs on it.
10. Remove the cakes from the oven and let them cool on racks for 15 minutes before removing them from the pans.
11. Let your cakes cool completely before trying to frost them. Sometimes I even refrigerate them for a brief time.
12. Place the first layer down and add about 1 cup of frosting, spread evenly over the top of the cake. Add rainbow sprinkles on top of the frosting.
13. Place the second layer on top and add 1 cup of frosting, spread evenly over the top of this second cake layer. Add more rainbow sprinkles.
14. Place the top layer on and put a thin layer of frosting over the entire cake, including the sides.
15. Place the cake in the refrigerator for at least 30 minutes to set.
16. Frost the rest of your cake with your buttercream and decorate as desired.

Ingredients

- 1 cup unsalted butter, room temperature
- 1¾ cups white sugar
- ⅓ cup vegetable oil
- 3 large eggs, room temperature
- ⅓ cup sour cream, room temperature
- 3 cups flour
- 1 Tbsp. baking powder
- 1 tsp. salt
- 1 cup whole-fat buttermilk, room temperature
- 1 Tbsp. vanilla or almond extract
- ⅓ cup rainbow sprinkles, to mix in cake batter, plus 1 cup for layering and decoration
- Homemade White Buttercream, recipe on page 121

Notes

Funfetti is a combination of fun and confetti! Pillsbury introduced the popular Funfetti cake in 1989.

In this recipe, you can switch out sprinkle colors to coincide with the holidays.

I use unsalted butter because it has less water content than salted butter and the water content can affect your batter.

Homemade White Buttercream

Makes 3½–4 cups

When I think about my top five favorite foods, buttercream is there! This is a family obsession—we love buttercream and a lot of it. This sweet, buttery, smooth frosting is the crown jewel to any baked dessert. Contrary to popular belief, buttercream does not always have to be super sweet. Offset that sweetness by adding ¼–½ tsp. of salt.

Ingredients

- 2 cups unsalted butter, chilled
- 6 cups powdered sugar
- 4–5 Tbsp. heavy cream
- 2 tsp. vanilla or almond extract

Instructions

1. In a mixing bowl or stand mixer, cream the butter for 2–3 minutes.

2. Turn the mixer to low speed and carefully add the powdered sugar 1 cup at a time. Mix well between additions.

3. Turn the mixer to medium speed and add the extract, salt, and heavy cream. I start with 4 Tbsp. of cream and add more as needed to reach my desired consistency.

4. Turn the mixer up to medium-high speed and let it beat for about 7 minutes. It will lighten up in color and texture.

CHAPTER 9

Beloved Beverages

On cold winter days, I'd wake my kids up for school and have a nice mug of hot chocolate waiting for them. There's nothing like a chocolate hug in the morning, and beverages are one of best ways to introduce young ones to the joys of mixing, blending, and concocting their own recipes.

page 131

page 124

page 125

page 21

page 127

page 126

Heart-Warming Hot Cocoa

Makes 8 servings

Nothing warms the soul and brings comfort like drinking a mug of creamy hot cocoa while covered with a fuzzy blanket. Loved as much by adults as kids, it takes us back to childhood memories and makes us smile from that first warm sip. Hot cocoa always takes me back to sledding down big Iowa hills with my snowy mittens and boots.

Ingredients

- 2 cups powdered sugar
- 1 cup unsweetened cocoa powder
- 2 cups powdered milk
- 1 tsp. salt
- ½–1 tsp. cayenne, optional

Instructions

1. Mix all the ingredients together in a large bowl and whisk them together, breaking up any lumps.
2. Store in an airtight container, away from humidity.
3. To serve, stir together ½ cup of the mix and ½ cup of hot water or milk for a rich and creamy drink.

Notes

The salt may seem odd, but it enhances the chocolate flavor.

Add cayenne if you want a little spicy kick in your hot cocoa.

Try elevating your hot cocoa with whipped cream, marshmallows, shaved chocolate, peppermint sticks, sprinkles, or caramel.

National Hot Chocolate Day is January 31.

Friendship Tea

Makes about 50 servings

This recipe was shared with me by a dear lady named Sylvia back in 1984. We had just moved to Des Moines, Iowa, and were managing an apartment complex. She resided there and befriended me, a young mother who was overwhelmed with moving, work, and small children. I will never forget her kindness and I treasure this recipe always.

Ingredients

- 2 cups orange drink mix, I use Tang
- 1 cup instant black tea
- 1 cup sugar
- ½ cup lemonade mix
- 1 tsp. cinnamon
- ½ tsp. cloves

Instructions

1. Mix all the ingredients together and store them in an airtight container.
2. Add 2–3 tsp. of the mixture to 8 oz. of hot water. If you prefer a stronger flavor, add another tsp. of tea mix.
3. Serve with a slice of lemon or orange on the side.

Notes

When packaged in small jars, this is a nice gift for teachers, friends, and neighbors.

The first astronaut to bring Tang into outer space was John Glenn in 1962.

For a little more flavor, add ½ tsp. allspice and ¼ tsp. nutmeg.

Creamy Chocolate Malt

Makes 3-4 servings

When I was a kid, every time my dad and I would go somewhere to eat, we ordered a chocolate malt. It did not matter if it was a local ice cream stand or a nicer restaurant, we placed our order and listened to the familiar sound of the mixer whirling our malts into creamy reality.

Ingredients

- ¾ cup whole milk or heavy cream
- ¼ cup malted milk powder
- 1 qt. chocolate ice cream
- Chocolate syrup, optional

Instructions

1. Put the milk and malt powder in the blender and blend well for about 1 minute.
2. Add the ice cream and continue blending, scraping the sides if needed.
3. For a richer chocolate flavor, add chocolate syrup.
4. Garnish as desired and serve right away.

Notes

You can use 1 qt. of vanilla ice cream and 5 Tbsp. of chocolate syrup as an alternative to chocolate ice cream.

I sometimes drizzle chocolate syrup on the inside of my clear serving cups for an extra chocolate blast!

Garnish with whipped cream, chocolate chips, cherries, sprinkles, or sweetened cocoa powder.

Oh! Oreo Malt

Makes 3-4 servings

I do not remember what made me put Oreos in a malt, but I did, and I'll never apologize for it. As if that crunchy and creamy filled cookie wasn't good enough on its own, this recipe adds blended ice cream, milk, and malt powder to create a sweet and creamy chocolaty dream.

Ingredients

- ¾ cup whole milk or heavy cream
- ¼ cup malted milk powder
- 1 qt. vanilla ice cream
- 25 Oreos, reserving 6–8 for garnish

Instructions

1. Put the milk and malt powder in the blender and blend well for about 1 minute.
2. Add the ice cream and continue blending, scraping the sides if needed.
3. Add the Oreos one at a time, using about 15–20. Do not overblend—it's ok to leave a few chunkier pieces.
4. Garnish with whipped cream and whole Oreos.

Notes

If you prefer a shake without the malted flavor, leave out the powdered malt.

You do not need to add chocolate syrup since the chocolate of the cookie will add plenty of chocolate flavor.

Malts are milkshakes, but milkshakes are not malts!

Adult Chocolate Peanut Butter Milkshake

Makes 3-4 servings

My husband Wade loves everything chocolate and peanut butter. So, when a friend introduced us to a delightful peanut butter whiskey, we knew it would perfectly pair with our homemade chocolate ice cream to make a decadent adult shake. Since Wade makes the ice cream for the café, we have VIP access for experimenting. It is a delicious and dangerous benefit!

Ingredients
- 1 cup whole milk or heavy cream
- 1 qt. chocolate ice cream
- 10 oz. peanut butter whiskey
- Whipped cream and peanut butter cup candy for garnish

Instructions
1. Put all the ingredients in the blender and blend on high for 2 minutes.
2. If it is too thick, add more milk. If it seems too thin, add more ice cream. Blend it again.
3. Garnish with whipped cream and chocolate peanut butter candy.

Notes

For a little more peanut butter flavor, add a few tablespoons of peanut butter.

Feel free to experiment with various adult add-ins like coffee liqueur, orange liqueur, banana liqueur, or chocolate liqueurs.

Milkshakes became popular in 1922 with the invention of the electric blender. It was not until 1937 that the straw was invented—so drinking a shake became much easier!

Pumpkin Affogato

Makes 1 serving

Hot, steamy coffee and cold, creamy ice cream are two opposites that bring me comfort. In this dessert drink, the sweet ice cream and the bitter coffee play well together. Honestly, who would not want their ice creamed drowned in coffee? It is the best of both worlds.

Ingredients

- 6–8 oz. strong brewed coffee or espresso
- 1–2 scoops pumpkin ice cream
- Whipped cream
- Dash of cinnamon

Instructions

1. Put scoops of pumpkin ice cream In a coffee mug.
2. Pour the hot coffee over the ice cream, add a dollop of whipped cream on top, and sprinkle with cinnamon.

Notes

Affogato is the Italian word for drowned, which is exactly what we do to that ice cream!

A traditional affogato is espresso poured over vanilla ice cream, but do not be afraid to experiment with flavors.

Hot Dr. Pepper

Makes 2 servings

My Dad was an avid Dr. Pepper memorabilia collector for years. If my memory serves me right, which is questionable, he found this recipe on a vintage Dr. Pepper poster he bought. No matter where it came from, it soon became a favorite in our house on Crestview Avenue, where the winters were cold and the Dr. Pepper was hot!

Ingredients

- 16 oz. Dr. Pepper
- Lemon slices
- Cinnamon stick, optional

Instructions

1. Warm the Dr. Pepper in a saucepan on the stove top until it's steaming.
2. Place a lemon slice or two in the bottom of a coffee mug, then pour the Dr. Pepper over the lemon. Let it steep with the lemon for a few minutes.
3. Garnish with a cinnamon stick, if desired.

Notes

In the 1960s, Dr. Pepper marketed itself as a hot holiday beverage alternative to hot ciders. The concoction was called "Devilishly Different" and a "Winter Warmer."

Warming up Dr. Pepper seems to highlight the secret 23 flavors in the mix.

CHAPTER 10

Favorites from My Chef Friends

I t's fun to surround yourself with wonderfully creative chefs who inspire and encourage one another. I'm fortunate to be able to call these chefs friends. They're a comfort to me in my business, and I know their recipes will comfort you and your family.

page 149

page 144

page 136

page 134

page 146

Bacon & Pimento Cheese Smash Burgers

Chef Chris Grove, Certified Food Judge for the World Food Championships and BBQ Cookbook Author

Makes 4 single smash burgers

There are several ways to make a burger, so what makes smash burgers unique? Smashing a ground beef ball on a hot metal surface creates the maximum crust, giving you maximum flavor. Flat-top griddles and cast-iron skillets are ideal cooking surfaces for a smash burger. This recipe is for single-patty burgers, but the wonderful thing about smash burgers is that it is easy to upsize them to doubles, triples, or larger by simply stacking the patties.

Ingredients

- 1 lb. fresh ground chuck
- 1–2 Tbsp. high-temperature cooking oil like peanut, canola, or avocado
- 1 tsp. seasoned salt, I used Morton's Season-All
- 8 slices cooked bacon, broken in half
- ½ cup pimento cheese (see Spicy Smoked Pimento Cheese recipe on page 91)
- 4 brioche hamburger buns, toasted on the cut sides
- Sliced tomato, lettuce leaves, sliced onions, or other toppings as desired

Instructions

1. Preheat a grill to 450-500°F. Ten minutes before cooking, place a grill-safe griddle or skillet on the grill grates. Alternatively, preheat a griddle over high heat.

2. Use a digital scale to divide the ground chuck into four 4-ounce portions and shape them into loosely formed balls.

3. Wipe or spray the griddle with cooking oil. Place a ball of beef on the griddle and use a burger press or spatula to smash the burger flat. Quickly repeat with the remaining balls of beef. Grill until the bottom of the patties is crusty, the edges turn grey, and juices begin to appear on top, about 3-4 minutes.

4. Flip the patties, season each with ¼ teaspoon of season salt, and top each with an ounce of pimento cheese. Cook until the bottom is crusty, and the cheese starts to melt, about 2-3 minutes. Remove from heat.

5. Top the bottom of the bun with lettuce, tomato, and onions. Top with a patty and four half-pieces of bacon. Top with bun and serve. If making a double or triple, repeat with more patties and bacon.

East Nashville Chicken & Dumplings

**Chef Dean Hitt, Founder of *Tennessee Cuisine*
and Owner of Tennessee Jacks on the Town**

Makes up to 20 servings

This recipe was imprinted on my mind by my mother's mother, who lived by herself in a sketchy (at the time) neighborhood of Northeast Nashville, until she was 102 years old. In my "coming-of-age" years, I spent my days and nights keeping her company, listening to her stories, and learning her recipes. This was her best comfort food recipe, which warmed the hearts and filled the bellies of several of us big boys who loved and respected her.

Ingredients

- 1 whole chicken
- 3 celery stalks, cut in half
- 1 small onion, chopped
- 3 carrots, chopped
- Poultry seasoning
- Fresh ground pepper
- 2 cups unbleached all-purpose flour, plus more for dusting the board
- 1 tsp. kosher salt, plus more for seasoning chicken
- 6 Tbsp. unsalted butter, very cold
- ¾ cup milk

Instructions

1. Remove and discard the giblets and neck from the chicken, if needed. Wash the chicken inside and out with cold water in the sink. Keep the chicken low in the sink to avoid splattering onto any surrounding surfaces to prevent contamination.
2. Place the chicken in a large pot and cover it with water at least 4" over the top of the chicken.
3. Add salt, pepper, poultry seasoning, celery, onion, and carrots to the pot.
4. Bring everything to a boil, then reduce the heat and simmer for 1 hour.
5. Remove from the heat and let cool. Using 2 large, slotted spoons, remove the chicken from the pot, place it in a colander in the sink, and continue cooling until the chicken is cool to the touch.
6. When the broth in the pot cools, strain it into large glass containers (I use an 8-cup clear glass measuring cup and several 1-quart canning jars). Refrigerate until fat collects at the top of containers.
7. After the chicken cools, carefully remove the meat from the bones. Place the meat in a large bowl and discard the bones.
8. Season the chicken with more salt and pepper and lightly chop it. Set it aside.
9. Combine the flour and 1 tsp. kosher salt in a bowl or in the bowl of a food processor.
10. Slice the butter into 1-Tbsp. chunks and cut the chunks into the flour until the mix resembles coarse meal. If you are using a food processor, just pulse until you achieve this consistency.
11. Add the milk and mix until well combined. Knead the dough a couple of times to tighten it up a bit, then turn it out onto a floured board or countertop.
12. Roll the dough out until it's about ⅛" thick.
13. Using a pizza cutter or sharp paring knife, cut the dough into ½"-wide strips. If you like, cut your strips to 4"–5" long (I drop whole strips into the boiling broth as that's how my grandmother did it). Set the strips aside.
14. Remove and discard the fat from the top of the broth in the containers. Pour the remaining broth into a large pot and bring it to a rolling boil.
15. Once the broth is boiling vigorously, drop the dough strips in one at a time. Once all the dough strips are added to the pot, reduce the heat and simmer for 15–20 minutes or until tender.
16. Once the dumplings are tender, add the chopped chicken to the pot and prepare to serve.

Notes

If your finished product is not thick enough for your taste, thicken the broth with a little bit of cornstarch and water once the dumplings are cooked. Just mix equal amounts together and add a little bit at a time until the broth reaches your desired consistency.

If you prefer a creamier broth, add a little bit of milk or heavy cream once the dumplings are cooked.

People think that dumplings are made from biscuit dough, and that is almost true. If you use biscuit dough containing baking powder and baking soda, when cooked, the dumplings will puff up and absorb too much broth, resulting in something closer to a chicken cobbler. Thus, the dumplings in this recipe are made without baking powder and baking soda.

Kimchi "Big Mac" with Gochujang Mayo

Chef Brandon Frohne,
Winner of Cooking Channel's
Snack Attack

Makes 1 sandwich

Instructions

1. Preheat the oven to 350°F.
2. Place the gochujang paste, ketchup, mayonnaise, garlic, and lime juice in a small mixing bowl. Mix well and set aside.
3. Place the bacon on a baking pan lined with parchment paper and cook 8–10 minutes. Remove the bacon from the oven and set it aside.
4. Make two slices in the brioche bun from the side so that it resembles a three-part Big Mac bun. Beat the egg white in a bowl, then lightly brush the top of the bun with it. Add a sprinkle of sesame seeds on top of the egg white. Bake in the oven for 5 minutes. Remove the bun from the oven and set it aside.
5. Heat a large cast-iron skillet over medium-high heat. Season the Wagyu patties on each side with salt and pepper. Drizzle ¼ cup of avocado oil into the skillet and place the patties on top. Place a burger weight on top of the patties and press down until they are ¼" thick. Cook 2 minutes on each side with the burger weight on top. Remove the burger weight and add an American cheese slice to each patty. Remove them from the pan and set them aside.
6. Toast the bun slices in the remaining fat/oil mixture in the cast-iron skillet until they are golden.
7. Place a spoonful of the gochujang mayonnaise on each bun slice. Then add the shredded lettuce, pickles, burger patties, bacon, kimchi, and scallions to bottom and middle layers of the bun slices.
8. Top with the bun "crown" and enjoy!

Ingredients

- 1 Tbsp. gochujang paste
- 1 Tbsp. ketchup
- ½ cup Duke's mayonnaise
- ½ Tbsp. chopped garlic
- Juice of 1 lime
- 2 strips of bacon
- 1 brioche bun
- 1 egg white
- 1 Tbsp. white sesame seeds
- Two 6-oz. Wagyu beef patties
- 1 cup shredded lettuce
- ¼ cup thinly sliced dill pickles
- 2 slices American cheese
- ¼ cup kimchi
- ¼ cup chopped scallions
- 2 tsp. kosher salt
- 2 tsp. cracked black pepper
- Avocado oil, as needed

Notes

Hands down this my go-to comfort fix! This burger combines my love for the fermented Korean condiment kimchi with the classic Big Mac burger! There's a certain beauty to holding this burger in your hands, smelling the smoky and spicy aromas, and watching the sauce drip down your arms while you stuff your face with this beast of a burger. Talk about nostalgia and comfort!

Shepherd's Pie Grilled Cheese

Chef Jen Bixby, Manager of It's All So Yummy Café

Makes 6 servings

This grilled cheese was one of our Grilled Cheese of the Month specials. We'd all been craving an ultimate comfort feeling and this was a natural choice.

Instructions

1. Add the oil to a large skillet on medium-high heat, then add the onions and cook them until they are soft.

2. Add the ground beef, parsley, rosemary, salt, and pepper and cook until the meat is browned. Add the Worcestershire sauce and garlic, and let it cook for 2 more minutes.

3. Add the flour and tomato paste and stir well to incorporate. Then add the broth and frozen vegetables and let the mixture come to a boil. Reduce the heat and simmer for 5–6 minutes until it thickens up a little. Set the mixture aside.

4. Put the diced potatoes in a large pot of water, making sure they are all covered. Bring to a boil and cook until the potatoes are tender, about 15 minutes.

5. Drain the potatoes and leave them in the hot pot. Add the butter, milk, garlic powder, salt, pepper, and sour cream and mash by hand or with a handheld electric mixer to your desired texture. Set them aside.

6. Heat the griddle to 350°F. Use a pastry brush to butter one side of each slice of bread and place them on the griddle buttered side down.

7. Put two slices of provolone cheese on each piece of bread. On half of the slices, add about ½ cup of mashed potatoes topped with about ½ cup of the meat mixture.

8. When the cheese has melted and the bread is golden brown, use a sturdy spatula to put the slices together.

9. Remove from the completed sandwiches from the griddle and sprinkle with parmesan cheese and parsley.

Ingredients

- 2 Tbsp. olive oil
- 1 yellow onion, chopped
- 1 lb. ground beef
- 1 tsp. dried parsley
- 1 tsp. rosemary
- ½–1 tsp. salt
- ½ tsp. black pepper
- 1½ Tbsp. Worcestershire sauce
- 2 fresh garlic cloves, minced
- 3 Tbsp. flour
- 3 Tbsp. tomato paste
- 1 cup beef broth
- 1 cup frozen mixed vegetables (green beans, corn, peas, and carrots)
- 2–3 large russet potatoes, peeled and cubed
- 1 stick butter
- ½ cup whole milk or half-and-half
- ½–1 tsp. garlic powder
- ½–1 tsp. salt
- ¼–½ tsp. black pepper
- ¼ cup sour cream
- 12 slices hearty bread
- 1 stick melted butter
- 24 slices provolone cheese
- Parmesan cheese and dried parsley, for serving

Notes

You can freeze the extra meat for future use or double the recipe and make a vegetable beef soup by adding tomato juice and beef stock!

Pasta Gnudi

**Chef Frank Aloise, Executive Chef
at Forest Creek Golf Club**

One of my family's favorite fun forms of "pasta" is a cheese-based dumpling called gnudi. My "famous" version of this deconstructed shell-less ravioli instantly melts in your mouth and has never disappointed. Although it pairs well with multiple sauces, I stick to my roots with an Italian staple, marinara. In true Sicilian fashion, my flare shows through with some added spice and a mild kick from Calabrian chili flakes, garlic, and fresh basil. It will satisfy everyone's tastebuds!

Ingredients

- 1 lb. ricotta cheese, preferably impastata (my favorite is Grande Cheese Company's Ricotta Del Pastaio)
- 2 eggs
- 2 cups grated imported Romano cheese
- ½ cup fine-shred Italian blend cheese (mozzarella and provolone)
- ¼ cup all-purpose flour, plus flour for rolling
- Pinch of sea salt
- ½ tsp. black pepper
- 1 tsp. granulated garlic
- ¼ cup fresh finely chopped Italian flat-leaf parsley

Instructions

1. Add all ingredients except for the flour to a mixer with a paddle attachment. On slow speed, blend the ingredients well and then slowly add the flour and let it mix for another minute. Assess the dough by pressing it with your finger. It should be tacky, but not wet or sticky. If the dough is too wet, slowly and gradually add more flour by the tablespoon until you reach the correct consistency. Do not add too much flour!

2. With a 1-oz. scoop or tablespoon, scoop a dollop of the dough and place it on a floured surface. Lightly flour your hands and place the dough ball in your palms. Roll it, keeping it round. Roll all the dough into balls.

3. In a large salted saucepan, bring water to a boil, then lower the heat to a slow simmer (not boiling).

4. Carefully place the gnudi into the pot one at a time without crowding or touching them. Only cook around 6 at a time. They will sink, then float after about 3–4 minutes. Once they float, carefully remove them with a slotted spoon.

5. Serve the gnudi hot with your favorite sauce.

Notes

If you won't be preparing all of the gnudi right away, freeze the remaining gnudi for another time. When freezing them, make sure they are generously coated with flour and remain loose and uncrowded on a flat surface (such as a sheet pan) until they are completely frozen.

I prefer gnudi with marinara, but you can serve them with any sauce. Try them with pesto or one of my other favorites, a mix of extra virgin olive oil, Parmigiano Reggiano, and fresh-cracked black pepper.

MoMo's Grilled Sausage & Pepper Sandwich

Chef Kevin Moreland, Chef and Owner of MoMo's Rhythm and Ribs Roadhouse Grill

Makes 6 servings

This is a house favorite twist on a classic Italian dish—grilled juicy sweet Italian sausage with tricolored peppers and red onions all piled high on a toasted brioche bun. It's hard to resist the urge to graze on this before it's all put together!

Instructions

1. Preheat your grill to medium-high.
2. Toss the peppers and onions in a bowl with ½ Tbsp. olive oil, salt, and pepper and set them aside.
3. Grill the sausages 12–15 mins or until done, turning to cook evenly on all sides. Once they are cooked, slice them into ½" medallions and set them aside
4. While the sausage is on the grill, transfer the vegetables to a grill basket and grill them for 10 mins, turning them occasionally with tongs so as not to burn them.
5. Preheat your oven to 425°F.
6. Place a heavy-bottomed Dutch oven or cast-iron skillet on a stovetop set to medium-high heat.
7. Melt together ½ Tbsp. olive oil and ½ Tbsp. butter, then add garlic and cook, stirring, for about 30 seconds until softened.
8. Add the sliced sausage and grilled vegetables, oregano, and basil, and cook, stirring, for 1 minute. Add the white wine and cook 3 more minutes until it cooks down and evaporates. Remove the mixture from the heat and toss in the parmesan cheese.
9. Butter both halves of the buns and place them butter side up on a cookie sheet in the oven. Bake for 2 minutes, then flip the buns upside down and cook for 2 more minutes. Remove them from the oven.
10. Add sausage mix on each bottom bun and top each with sliced provolone. Return the topped bottom buns only to the oven and cook until the cheese is melted, about 2 minutes.
11. Remove the bottoms from the oven and finish with the bun tops.

Ingredients

- 1 lb. sweet Italian sausages
- 1 Tbsp. olive oil, divided
- 2 Tbsp. butter, divided
- 1 red bell pepper, seeds removed and sliced
- 1 yellow bell pepper, seeds removed and sliced
- 1 green bell pepper, seeds removed and sliced
- 1 red onion, sliced
- 2 cloves garlic, minced
- ½ cup dry white wine
- ½ tsp. kosher salt
- ½ tsp. freshly ground black pepper
- 1 Tbsp. fresh oregano, chopped
- 1 Tbsp. fresh basil, chopped
- 2 Tbsp. grated parmesan cheese
- 6 fresh brioche buns
- 6 slices provolone cheese

Blackberry Pie

Chef Lisa Varnado, Founder of Marble City Sweets

Makes one 9" pie

This blackberry pie is amazing during the summer, but the warming spices make it the perfect dessert all year round!

Instructions

1. Place the flour, salt, and sugar into a food processor and pulse just until combined.

2. Add butter to the food processor and pulse several times until the butter chunks are no larger than peas.

3. Slowly add the ice-cold water and vinegar mixture. Pulse between each addition of water until the dough just starts to hold together when pinched between two fingers. You may not need all the water.

4. Turn the crumbly dough out onto your work surface, form two equal-size mounds, and wrap each tightly in plastic wrap to form discs. Chill the dough for at least 2 hours.

5. Remove the dough from the refrigerator and let it sit for 5 minutes. Roll out the first disc of dough on a floured surface into a large circle and transfer it to a pie tin. Press the dough into your pie tin, fold the excess dough under itself, and flute the edges using your thumb and forefinger, or by pressing down with a fork. Chill or freeze until you are ready to bake.

6. Puree 2 cups of the blackberries in a blender until they form a liquid. Strain out the seeds and pour into a saucepan. Whisk in 1¼ cups of sugar. Cook over medium heat until the mixture is boiling, stirring constantly to prevent it from sticking to the bottom of the pan. Keep at a boil for 5 minutes, then remove from the heat.

7. Mix cornstarch and wine in a cup. When well mixed, whisk into the pan, turn the heat back on and stir until mixture returns to a boil. Remove from heat and stir in the spices. The mixture should resemble a thin pudding.

8. Fill your pie shell with the remaining 2 cups of blackberries. Pour the blackberry puree over the fresh berries, covering evenly.

9. Roll out the remaining dough and cut into even 1" strips. Weave the strips into a lattice over top of the blackberry filling. Trim any strips that overhang the sides.

10. Brush the top of the pie with an egg wash and sprinkle with sugar.

11. Bake at 400°F for 20 minutes. Drop the tempeartures to 350°F and cook for an additional 30 minutes.

Ingredients

- 2½ cups all-purpose flour, plus extra for rolling
- 1 tsp. salt
- 8 oz. unsalted butter, cold and cubed
- 1 tsp. sugar
- ¼–½ cup ice water with a splash of white vinegar stirred in
- 4 cups fresh blackberries, divided
- 1¼ cups sugar, plus 1 Tbsp.
- ¼ cup cornstarch
- 2 Tbsp. dry white wine with high acidity
- 1 tsp. nutmeg
- 1 Tbsp. cinnamon
- 1 Tbsp. white sugar
- 1 egg, whisked with a splash of heavy cream, for egg wash

Hummingbird Cake

**Chef Tee Dedrick, Founder of
Special Tee Cookies & Catering**

Makes 12 servings

Several years ago, I was searching for popular
Southern cakes and discovered Hummingbird
Cake. Exactly how this cake got its name isn't
clear, but it definitely has something to do with
its flavor, which is sure to suit any nectar-loving
hummingbirds and really anyone with a love
of sweet desserts. This celebration of tropical
fruits and nuts first appeared in *Southern
Living* magazine in 1978. It's since become a
signature cake of the South and my new favorite
comfort cake.

Ingredients

- 1 cup chopped pecans
- 3 cups all-purpose flour
- 1½ cups sugar
- 1½ tsp. ground cinnamon
- 1 tsp. salt
- 1 tsp. baking soda
- ⅛ tsp. fresh ground nutmeg
- 3 large eggs, lightly beaten
- 1½ cups vegetable oil
- 1½ tsp. vanilla extract, plus 1 Tbsp. for the frosting
- 3 cups chopped bananas (about 4 medium bananas)
- One 8-oz. can crushed pineapple in juice
- 2 sticks lightly salted butter
- One 8-oz. package cream cheese
- 8 cups powdered sugar

Instructions

1. Preheat the oven to 350°F. Bake the pecans in a single layer in a shallow pan for 6 to 8 minutes or until they are toasted and fragrant, stirring halfway through.

2. Coat three 9" round cake pans with flour and cooking spray.

3. Whisk together the flour, sugar, cinnamon, salt, baking soda, and nutmeg in a large bowl. Add the eggs, oil, and 1½ tsp. of the vanilla, and stir just until the dry ingredients are moistened. Fold in the bananas, pineapple, and pecans. The batter will be very thick, more like banana bread batter than cake batter.

4. Spoon the batter into the prepared pans. Bake at 350°F for 28 to 30 minutes. Cool in the pans on a wire rack for 10 minutes, then remove the cakes from the pans and place directly on the wire rack to cool completely (about 30 minutes).

5. While the cake cools, cream the butter and cream cheese in a mixing bowl until incorporated. With the mixer on low, add the remaining vanilla and the powdered sugar, continuing to mix until the frosting is smooth and spreadable.

6. Place 1 cake layer on a cake stand or serving plate and top it with ¼ of the frosting. Add the second cake layer and top it with ¼ of the frosting. Top the second layer with the remaining cake and evenly spread the remaining frosting over the top and sides of the cake.

Night at the Movies Ice Cream

Chef Wade Wilcox, Owner of It's All So Yummy Café

Makes 1 quart

Are you a buttery popcorn and M&M's mixed together moviegoer? I went a step further and churned this sweet and salty mix into ice cream! Stream your favorite movie, grab a soft blanket, curl up on the couch, and enjoy this movie-night treat at home.

Ingredients

- Vanilla Ice Cream, recipe on page 116
- 1 bag of extra-butter popcorn, popped
- One 10.7-oz. bag M&M's

Instructions

1. Make the Vanilla Ice Cream recipe on page 116. Once you've reached step 5 and your mix has cooled to 65°F, put it in a large bowl and add the popcorn. Stir it in well, making sure that the popcorn is saturated. Let the mix sit for at least 3 hours, stirring occasionally. Assess the popcorn flavor—if you want more, let it sit for another hour.

2. Once the base has a good popcorn flavor, use a cheesecloth to strain the milk, leaving the popcorn behind.

3. Pour the mixture into to your ice cream maker and churn according to your machine's instructions.

4. When you transfer the ice cream into a large bowl to freeze, stir in the M&M's, saving a handful for garnish.

Notes

Using good, extra-buttery popcorn will enhance the flavor of your ice cream.

Hot Pepper Fudge

Chefs Chris and Allyson Virden, Founders of Olde Virden's Tennessee Pepper Co.

Makes 50 small squares

Chocolate and chilis were made for each other! These sweet, salty, spicy squares are perfect after-dinner or party treats.

Ingredients

- 1 stick butter
- 1 box powdered sugar
- ¼ tsp. sea salt
- ¼ cup milk
- ½ cup cocoa powder
- 1 tsp. vanilla
- A little less than ½ tsp. fine chili pepper blend (we use Olde Virden's Red Hot Fine Grind)

Instructions

1. Put all the ingredients in a pot on the stove. Heat over medium heat until all the ingredients are melted and mixed well.
2. Stir until smooth. Pour the mixture into a 1–1½-qt. baking dish lined with wax paper. Chill for 20 minutes in the freezer, then cut into small squares and enjoy.

Notes

Add more chili pepper blend if you want your fudge to be spicier.

Cold Brew with Aggressive Strawberry Cold Foam

Chefs Amy and Adam Kennedy and Chad Greenor, Founders and Owners of Refill Coffee Cart

Makes 1 serving

The first step to this recipe is to make our Aggressive Strawberry Cold Foam, which we deem to be "aggressive" because it also contains our cold brew coffee! Typically, cold foam doesn't have any added caffeine power.

Ingredients

- 4 Tbsp. cold brew coffee, plus as much as you want for your drink
- 4 Tbsp. heavy whipping cream
- 4 Tbsp. strawberry syrup
- Ice

Instructions

1. Add the 4 Tbsp. of cold brew coffee, heavy whipping cream, and strawberry syrup to a blender. Blend together for at least 15 seconds. You want the blend to be creamy and thick but not so thick that it won't easily pour out of the blender. Let the cold foam sit in the blender for a moment.

2. Put as much glass in a 12-oz. glass as you prefer, then fill the glass halfway with cold brew coffee.

3. Pour the Aggressive Strawberry Cold Foam over the cold brew and ice. You should see a clear separation in the glass as the cold foam sits on top of the cold brew.

Notes

Watching the cold foam slowly mix down into the cold brew is fun and pretty rad! It's ok if you want to speed up the process by stirring your drink, though.

Recipe CONVERSIONS

Many recipes in this book use volume-based ingredients and can be converted to their metric volume equivalent (given below). If you would rather convert to mass (grams), you should research the correct conversion for the exact ingredient being measured, since different ingredients have different masses.

⅛ **teaspoon** = 0.6 mL	½ **cup** = 120 mL
¼ **teaspoon** = 1.2 mL	¾ **cup** = 175 mL
½ **teaspoon** = 2.5 mL	**1 cup** = 240 mL
1 teaspoon = 5 mL	**1 fluid ounce** = 30 mL
½ **tablespoon** = 7.5 mL	**1 ounce** = 28 grams
1 tablespoon = 15 mL	**1 fluid pound** = 500 mL
⅛ **cup** = 30 mL	**1 pound** = 453 grams
¼ **cup** = 60 mL	

About the Author

Kim Wilcox is a renowned chef and restaurant owner of the family owned and operated It's All So Yummy Café in Knoxville, Tennessee. For more than ten years, It's All So Yummy Café has been serving residents homemade soups, salads, sandwiches, ice cream, and their most famous specialty, savory and unique grilled cheese sandwiches. Beginning in 2009, Kim started her business with just one cake on the menu. It has since grown and evolved, and Kim's restaurant has since been featured on the Food Network, the Cooking Channel, and local news programs. An inventive and out-of-the-box chef, Kim is the author of *Great Book of Grilled Cheese* and also appeared in the best-selling book *The Ultimate SPAM® Cookbook*, contributing two of her original recipes. To learn more about Kim and her restaurant, visit *www.ItsAllSoYummy.com*, or their Facebook (@itsallsoyummycafe) and Instagram (@itsallsoyummycafeowner) pages.

Acknowledgments

I would like to thank my friends, family, and my husband Wade for their support and encouragement as this book came together. We've had numerous conversations and walks down memory lane as we talk about comfort food and what it means to each other. Thank you for sharing your heartwarming stories and memories with me, it shows how deep the history of comfort food is.

I've very much enjoyed this journey and I hope that this cookbook makes you reminiscence for a moment and inspires you to create new memories.

Many thanks again to Chris Grove, my friend, mentor, and photographer. We had many good laughs, several early mornings, and more energy drinks than we should have. It's an honor to work with you again and my great fortune to be friends with you.

About the Contributors

Frank Aloise, Executive Chef at Forest Creek Golf Club

Frank Aloise's love and passion for food comes from his childhood memories growing up in a large Sicilian family back home in Boston, Massachusetts.

After moving to Knoxville in 2010, Frank worked for The Copper Cellar corporation as executive chef. In 2015, he relaunched the opening of one of their flagship restaurants, Cappuccino's, which propelled his career in so many ways.

Frank now resides in Pinehurst, North Carolina, with his family, where he is the executive chef of Forest Creek Golf Club. Today, Frank is doing what he loves as an entrepreneur, working as a private/freelance chef and restaurant consultant and currently working on a new project and venture, coming soon.

"We will meet thousands of people in our lifetime, most whom we will forget, but you will always remember the scent and taste of an amazing meal!" Frank has been blessed with all his senses and the skills to use them, and he believes that's what makes a great chef!

Connect with Frank on Instagram @cheffrankaloise

Jen Bixby, Manager of It's All So Yummy Café

Cooking has always been a fiery passion that burns deep down in Jen Bixby's soul. As a young girl, she would often stand beside her mother and father while they cooked, watching and learning, and probably getting in the way! She asked many questions and was mesmerized by the process of plating a beautiful meal that fed the people you love the most. She saw (and sees) cooking as the ultimate act of love.

As she grew older, she worked her way through many kitchens. Within those kitchens, she learned every position in a restaurant that you could possibly learn. She wanted to understand the restaurant business from every point of view, including the business aspect. In the midst of doing this, she also took jobs in many different cuisines, learning as much as she could. Any type of food is her type of food, and she took pride in learning every cuisine inside and out.

Jen takes a lot of pride in her skills because cooking is her passion. To her, there is nothing better in this world than being able to feed the people you love—to feed people is to love them from the deepest parts of your soul. Every time she cooks for someone, she shares a part of herself with that person. There is still much to learn and much growing to do, but as long as there is breath in her, she will work hard every day to become a better chef.

Connect with Jen on Instagram @animus405

Tee Dedrick, Founder of Special Tee Cookies & Catering

Tee Dedrick was born in Newtown, Connecticut, where the kitchen was the heart of the home and the place everyone gathered to pitch in and cook wonderful holiday meals together. Tee's Polish grandmother always had a task for everyone. It wasn't until her teenage years that she found a love of baking that soon grew into her love language. Seeing the joy her cooking brought to people really warmed her heart and motivated her. Tee gave her cookies to new visitors in her Sunday school class, and people would ask why she didn't sell them. When her husband became disabled in 2008, she started a cookie business. She continues to build her culinary skills and has been fortunate to have a successful bakery and catering business in Knoxville, Tennessee, where she resides with her husband. She has been featured in cooking segments on local television for over ten years.

Connect with Tee on Instagram @specialteecookiescatering

Brandon Frohne, Winner of Cooking Channel's Snack Attack

Chef Brandon Frohne uses influences from his European and Southern roots in his approach to contemporary American cuisine. With a commitment to sourcing ingredients from neighboring farms and local artisans, Brandon creates seasonally influenced dishes enriched with his creative culinary style and a pop of global flavor.

A fourth-generation chef, you could say that Brandon was born to create great food. It's in his Southern DNA. At 34 years old, he's risen quickly to the top as a nationally recognized, award-winning chef. His culinary creativity has been recognized by local and national press, including *Forbes Travel*, *Southern Living*, *Taste of the South*, *Every Day with Rachael Ray*, *Garden & Gun*, and more. Brandon has made television appearances on Food Network's *Chopped* and *Chopped Redemption*, Travel Channel's *Chow Masters* and *Secret Eats*, and, most recently, was the winner of Cooking Channel's *Snack Attack* in 2020.

Connect with Brandon on Instagram @brandon_frohne

Chris Grove, Certified Food Judge for the World Food Championships and BBQ Cookbook Author

BBQ and grilling author Chris Grove found his passion for BBQ when he had his first bite of pulled pork as a barefoot 7-year-old on his grandparents' North Carolina farm. In 2008, that fire led him to create the popular BBQ and grilling blog, Nibble Me This, to document his pursuit of getting that perfect BBQ bite. Chris is the pitmaster of his award-winning competition team, which has cooked at BBQ competitions, food festivals, and charity events around the country. When not competing in food sport, Chris is also a certified food judge for the Kansas City BBQ Society, Steak Cookoff Association, and World Food Championships. Chris has developed recipes for well-known brands for over a decade and his work has been featured in national media, including the cover of *Tailgating Magazine*. Chris met Kim as a frequent customer at her café, and they became friends through their mutual love for delicious, homemade comfort food.

Connect with Chris on Instagram @nibblemethis

Dean Hitt, Founder of *Tennessee Cuisine* and Owner of Tennessee Jacks on the Town

Born in Nashville, Tennessee, Dean grew up in an environment that encouraged achievement and creativity. Later, while immersed in the academic world, Dean began to yearn for the excitement of the commercial world. He found comfort in a small jazz bar and fine-dining restaurant in Knoxville's bohemian Old City. His entrepreneurial spirit took hold, and in 1986 he became a partner in that business. It was this venture that led him to pioneer the first trade magazine for the restaurant industry in the state of Tennessee, *Entree*, which he published for nine years.

While developing and promoting a cookbook with local celebrity Chef Jock, Dean used his background in television production and his magazine's extensive library of copy to create a 30-minute culinary video magazine. The first episode of *Tennessee Cuisine* premiered on CBS affiliate WVLT-TV on September 25, 1999.

In August of 2001, Chef Jock was seriously injured in an accident that brought *Tennessee Cuisine* to a halt. The tragedy of September 11 followed on the heels of Chef Jock's accident, and the negative economic impact resulted in the suspension of publication of *Entree*. Currently, Dean dedicates his time to his restaurant, Tennessee Jacks on the Town, in Morristown, Tennessee.

Connect with Dean on Instagram @mtnrover

Amy and Adam Kennedy and Chad Greenor, Founders and Owners of Refill Coffee Cart

Refill Coffee Cart is a tiny, mobile coffee cart that provides caffeinated catering, whole bean, and cold brew coffee. We offer coffee catering all over East Tennessee, cold brew delivery in the Knoxville, Tennessee area and ship whole bean coffee all over the United States.

Our coffee carts are small enough to fit indoors but fully capable of operating outdoors, making them very versatile additions to any event. Our carts have been designed so that they can fit into corners, lobbies, porches, break rooms, and more, while leaving plenty of room for you and your guests to socialize and celebrate.

Connect with Refill Coffee Cart on Instagram @refillcoffeecart

Kevin Moreland, Owner of MoMo's Rhythm and Ribs Roadhouse Grill

Chef Mo began his culinary career as a way to pay for college. While attending the University of Iowa, he learned every aspect of the restaurant industry and developed a passion for hospitality that still fuels him today. After graduation, Mo left for Los Angeles to work in the entertainment business for a few years before moving back to the Midwest to marry his college sweetheart. The couple moved to Chicago, where Mo reignited his affection for food service by studying under James Beard winner Jean JoHo (Brasserie Jo) and Cajun cuisine master Jimmy Bannos (Heaven on Seven). As the Moreland family began to expand, Chef Mo moved back to his native Iowa and opened his critically acclaimed Kin Folks Texas Style BBQ. He shuttered Kin Folks during the recession as the schedule took too much away from spending formative years with his wife and four children.

MoMo's Rhythm and Ribs Roadhouse Grill is a catering company that began by providing free meals to those affected by the COVID-19 pandemic. This labor of love combined two of his passions: hospitality and being of service to others. Even though the pandemic's impact continues to lessen, to this day Chef Mo is active with organizations like The Leukemia Lymphoma Society and Ronald McDonald House, and continues to do what he does best: providing "food hugs" to those in need.

Connect with Kevin on Instagram @mos_ribs

Lisa Varnado, Founder of Marble City Sweets

Lisa is a passionate, scratch-baking cake and sugar artist in Knoxville, Tennessee, specializing in over-the-top custom cakes and gourmet desserts. After graduating from The University of Tennessee Culinary Institute in 2012, Lisa held various jobs within the food industry. She is now a Culinary Arts Instructor at The Rel Maples Institute for Culinary Arts, as well as the founder of Marble City Sweets, a custom cake and edible art bakery. Lisa has always loved cooking, baking, and creating gourmet desserts that look like pieces of art. She started Marble City Sweets in 2017 and has been busy making delectable desserts ever since. Lisa has won countless awards for her cakes, and she recently competed on *Sugar Rush* on Netflix. She's living her dream!

Connect with Lisa on Instagram and Facebook @marblecitysweets

Chris and Allyson Virden, Founders of Olde Virden's Tennessee Pepper Co.

Olde Virden's Red Hot Sprinkle is the brainchild of Chris Virden. The idea came to him while operating a hike-in lodge on top of Mt. LeConte in the Great Smoky Mountains National Park with his wife Allyson. He felt there needed to be a better option for pizza than the generic red pepper flake found in every pizza restaurant in America. So Chris set off on a mission to create a perfect blend of five different chili peppers.

Olde Virden's sources their peppers from local Tennessee farmers and manufactures the sprinkle in their small family-run facility in Knoxville. The pepper blend is a healthy and delicious alternative to hot sauce that is free of sodium, sugar, additives, or preservatives. Olde Virden's is unique in the sense that it is made in small batches. The peppers are dehydrated the same day they are picked up from the farm and the product is shipped within a week of being bottled. Small-batch processing guarantees their product is fresh. Red Hot Sprinkle is a versatile pepper blend that can be added to eggs, chili, spaghetti sauce, dry rubs, deviled eggs, gumbo, cocktails, and even fudge. Olde Virden's brings a great flavor and a pleasant amount of heat to any dish.

Connect with Old Virden's Tennessee Pepper Co. on Instagram @olde_virdens

Wade Wilcox, Owner of It's All So Yummy Café

Wade Wilcox is known as the Ice Cream Man at It's All So Yummy Café. Wade completed the prestigious 119-year-old Penn State Ice Cream Short Course! Each year, about 120 students from all over the world are chosen to attend the program. Throughout this intensive week of training, Wade added to the knowledge and expertise he's gained since the café opened in 2011. He now has new techniques and plenty of science tools in his arsenal to develop even more creative, delicious frozen treats. He's also expanded the café's small-batch ice cream equipment to better serve custom ice cream needs and create out-of-this-world seasonal and fun ice cream flavors.

Index

Photo Credits

The following images are credited to Shutterstock.com and their respective creators: page 7 cast iron: Michael C. Gray; page 8 hand mixer: MicrostockStudio; page 9 tea towels: Nuoveenergie; page 9 bowls and dessert cups: MaraZe; pages 12, 22, 34, 58, 74, 100, 122, and 132 food icons: bioraven; page 28 cornmeal: HandmadePictures; page 46 sandwich icon: Artco; page 53 pickled onions: Kim Miller Media; page 68 mashed potatoes: DronG; page 116 ice cream: Natalia Lisovskaya; page 142 gnudi: Josef Volsa; page 151 cutting board: Guiyuan Chen; page 151 striped background: Donnay Style.